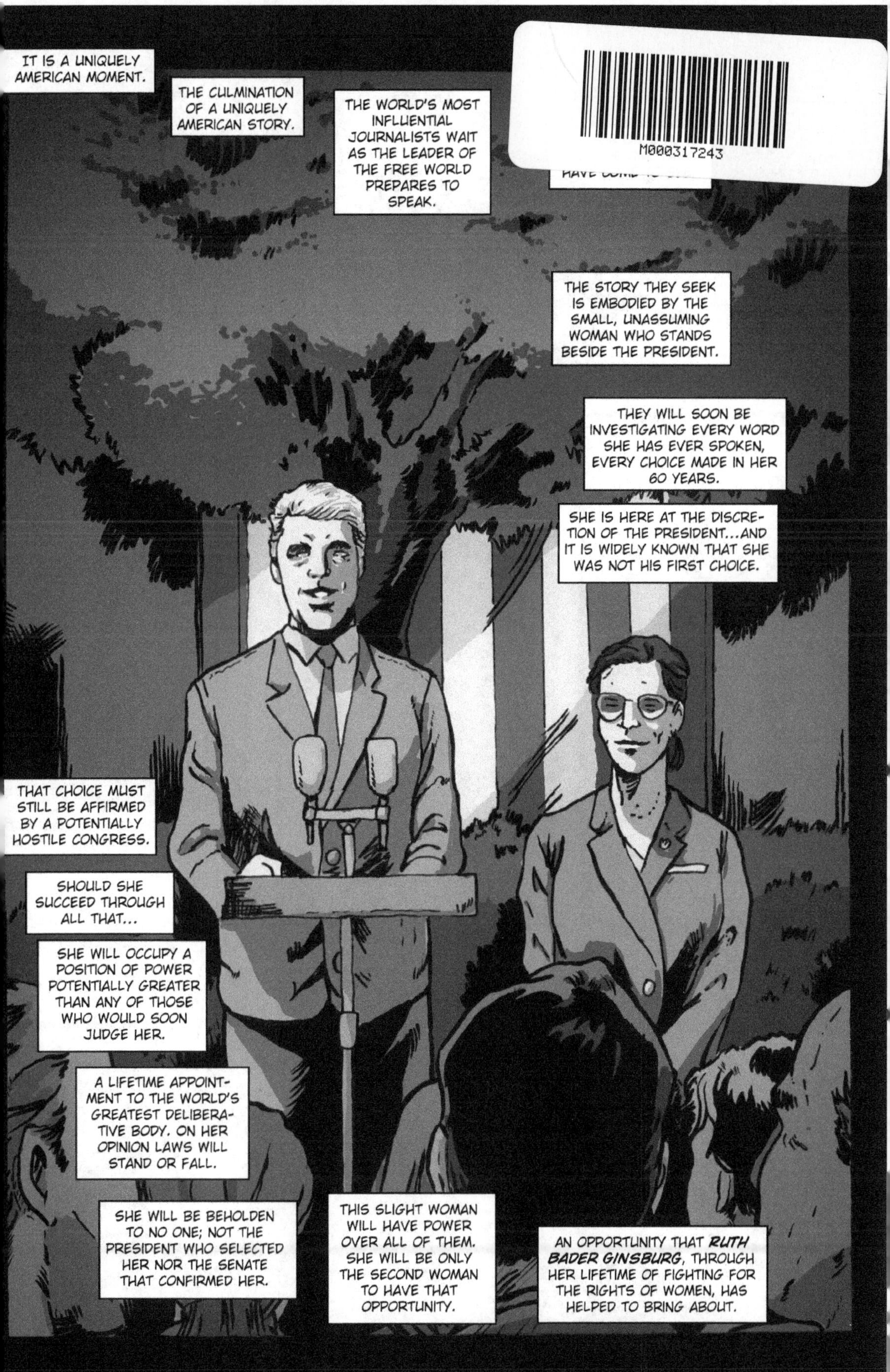
IT IS A UNIQUELY AMERICAN MOMENT.
THE CULMINATION OF A UNIQUELY AMERICAN STORY.
THE WORLD'S MOST INFLUENTIAL JOURNALISTS WAIT AS THE LEADER OF THE FREE WORLD PREPARES TO SPEAK.
THE STORY THEY SEEK IS EMBODIED BY THE SMALL, UNASSUMING WOMAN WHO STANDS BESIDE THE PRESIDENT.
THEY WILL SOON BE INVESTIGATING EVERY WORD SHE HAS EVER SPOKEN, EVERY CHOICE MADE IN HER 60 YEARS.
SHE IS HERE AT THE DISCRETION OF THE PRESIDENT...AND IT IS WIDELY KNOWN THAT SHE WAS NOT HIS FIRST CHOICE.
THAT CHOICE MUST STILL BE AFFIRMED BY A POTENTIALLY HOSTILE CONGRESS.
SHOULD SHE SUCCEED THROUGH ALL THAT...
SHE WILL OCCUPY A POSITION OF POWER POTENTIALLY GREATER THAN ANY OF THOSE WHO WOULD SOON JUDGE HER.
A LIFETIME APPOINTMENT TO THE WORLD'S GREATEST DELIBERATIVE BODY. ON HER OPINION LAWS WILL STAND OR FALL.
SHE WILL BE BEHOLDEN TO NO ONE; NOT THE PRESIDENT WHO SELECTED HER NOR THE SENATE THAT CONFIRMED HER.
THIS SLIGHT WOMAN WILL HAVE POWER OVER ALL OF THEM. SHE WILL BE ONLY THE SECOND WOMAN TO HAVE THAT OPPORTUNITY.
AN OPPORTUNITY THAT *RUTH BADER GINSBURG*, THROUGH HER LIFETIME OF FIGHTING FOR THE RIGHTS OF WOMEN, HAS HELPED TO BRING ABOUT.

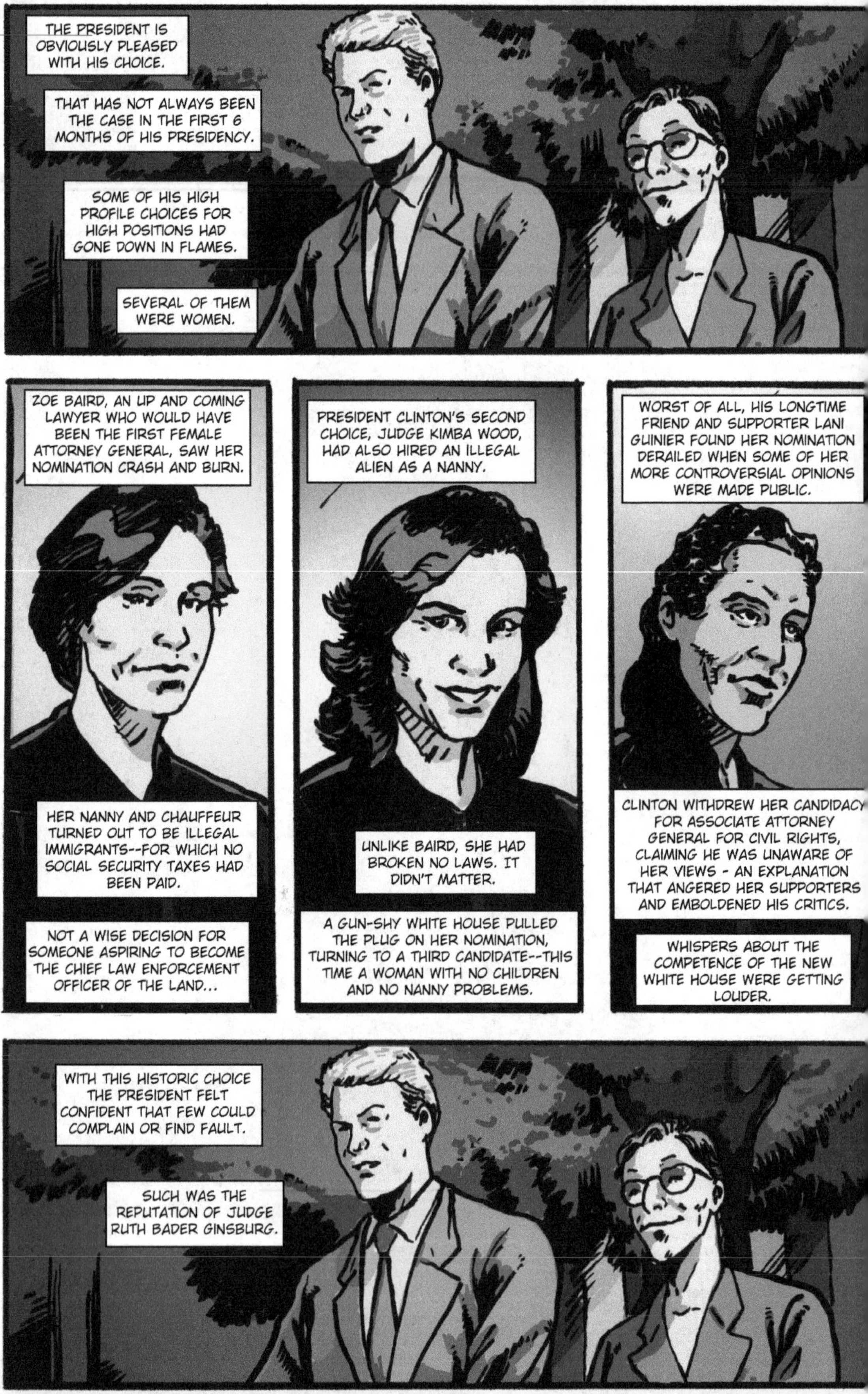
THE PRESIDENT IS OBVIOUSLY PLEASED WITH HIS CHOICE.
THAT HAS NOT ALWAYS BEEN THE CASE IN THE FIRST 6 MONTHS OF HIS PRESIDENCY.
SOME OF HIS HIGH PROFILE CHOICES FOR HIGH POSITIONS HAD GONE DOWN IN FLAMES.
SEVERAL OF THEM WERE WOMEN.
ZOE BAIRD, AN UP AND COMING LAWYER WHO WOULD HAVE BEEN THE FIRST FEMALE ATTORNEY GENERAL, SAW HER NOMINATION CRASH AND BURN.
HER NANNY AND CHAUFFEUR TURNED OUT TO BE ILLEGAL IMMIGRANTS--FOR WHICH NO SOCIAL SECURITY TAXES HAD BEEN PAID.
NOT A WISE DECISION FOR SOMEONE ASPIRING TO BECOME THE CHIEF LAW ENFORCEMENT OFFICER OF THE LAND...
PRESIDENT CLINTON'S SECOND CHOICE, JUDGE KIMBA WOOD, HAD ALSO HIRED AN ILLEGAL ALIEN AS A NANNY.
UNLIKE BAIRD, SHE HAD BROKEN NO LAWS. IT DIDN'T MATTER.
A GUN-SHY WHITE HOUSE PULLED THE PLUG ON HER NOMINATION, TURNING TO A THIRD CANDIDATE--THIS TIME A WOMAN WITH NO CHILDREN AND NO NANNY PROBLEMS.
WORST OF ALL, HIS LONGTIME FRIEND AND SUPPORTER LANI GUINIER FOUND HER NOMINATION DERAILED WHEN SOME OF HER MORE CONTROVERSIAL OPINIONS WERE MADE PUBLIC.
CLINTON WITHDREW HER CANDIDACY FOR ASSOCIATE ATTORNEY GENERAL FOR CIVIL RIGHTS, CLAIMING HE WAS UNAWARE OF HER VIEWS - AN EXPLANATION THAT ANGERED HER SUPPORTERS AND EMBOLDENED HIS CRITICS.
WHISPERS ABOUT THE COMPETENCE OF THE NEW WHITE HOUSE WERE GETTING LOUDER.
WITH THIS HISTORIC CHOICE THE PRESIDENT FELT CONFIDENT THAT FEW COULD COMPLAIN OR FIND FAULT.
SUCH WAS THE REPUTATION OF JUDGE RUTH BADER GINSBURG.

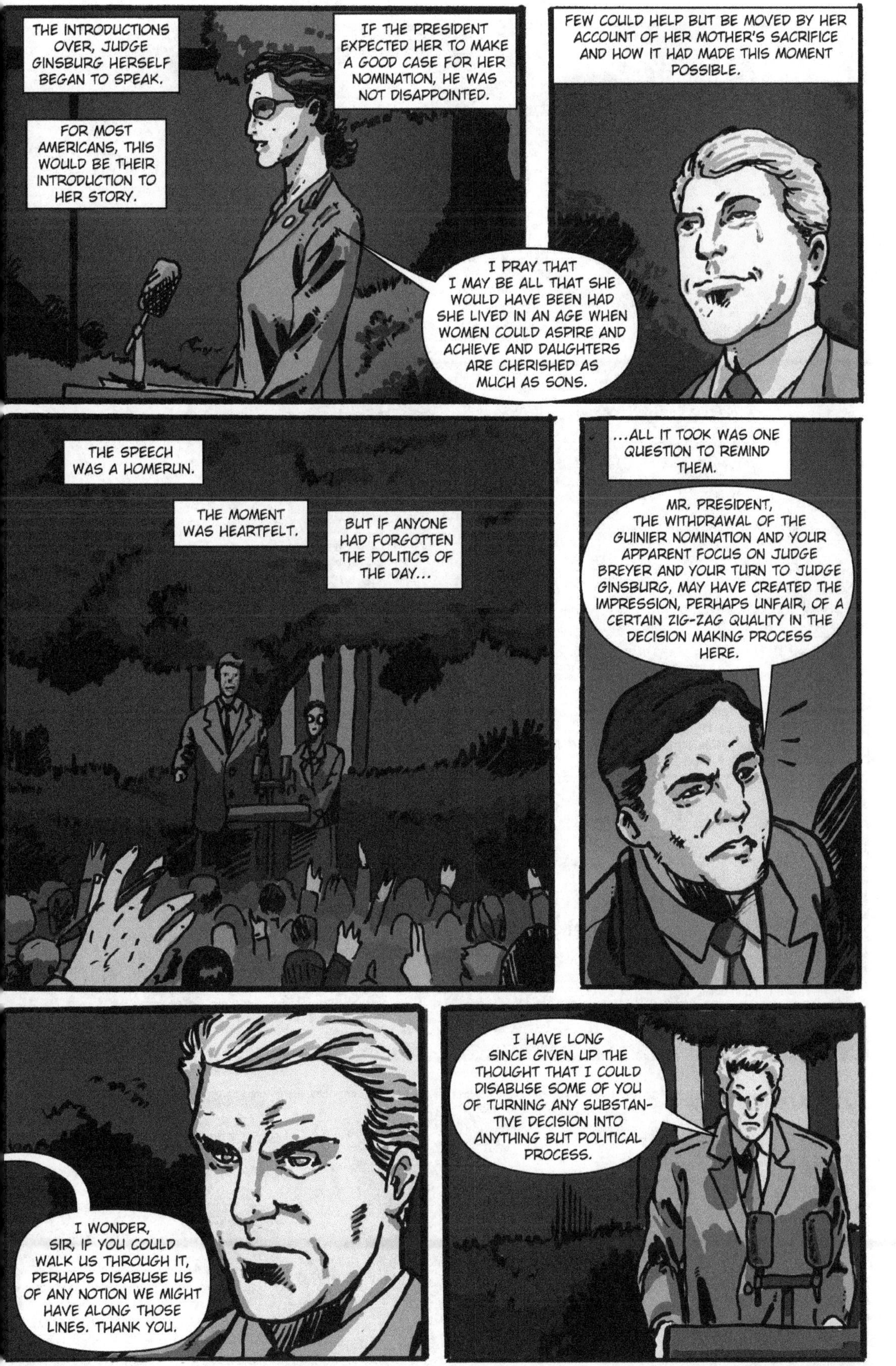
THE INTRODUCTIONS OVER, JUDGE GINSBURG HERSELF BEGAN TO SPEAK.
FOR MOST AMERICANS, THIS WOULD BE THEIR INTRODUCTION TO HER STORY.
IF THE PRESIDENT EXPECTED HER TO MAKE A GOOD CASE FOR HER NOMINATION, HE WAS NOT DISAPPOINTED.
I PRAY THAT I MAY BE ALL THAT SHE WOULD HAVE BEEN HAD SHE LIVED IN AN AGE WHEN WOMEN COULD ASPIRE AND ACHIEVE AND DAUGHTERS ARE CHERISHED AS MUCH AS SONS.
FEW COULD HELP BUT BE MOVED BY HER ACCOUNT OF HER MOTHER'S SACRIFICE AND HOW IT HAD MADE THIS MOMENT POSSIBLE.
THE SPEECH WAS A HOMERUN.
THE MOMENT WAS HEARTFELT.
BUT IF ANYONE HAD FORGOTTEN THE POLITICS OF THE DAY...
...ALL IT TOOK WAS ONE QUESTION TO REMIND THEM.
MR. PRESIDENT, THE WITHDRAWAL OF THE GUINIER NOMINATION AND YOUR APPARENT FOCUS ON JUDGE BREYER AND YOUR TURN TO JUDGE GINSBURG, MAY HAVE CREATED THE IMPRESSION, PERHAPS UNFAIR, OF A CERTAIN ZIG-ZAG QUALITY IN THE DECISION MAKING PROCESS HERE.
I WONDER, SIR, IF YOU COULD WALK US THROUGH IT, PERHAPS DISABUSE US OF ANY NOTION WE MIGHT HAVE ALONG THOSE LINES. THANK YOU.
I HAVE LONG SINCE GIVEN UP THE THOUGHT THAT I COULD DISABUSE SOME OF YOU OF TURNING ANY SUBSTAN-TIVE DECISION INTO ANYTHING BUT POLITICAL PROCESS.

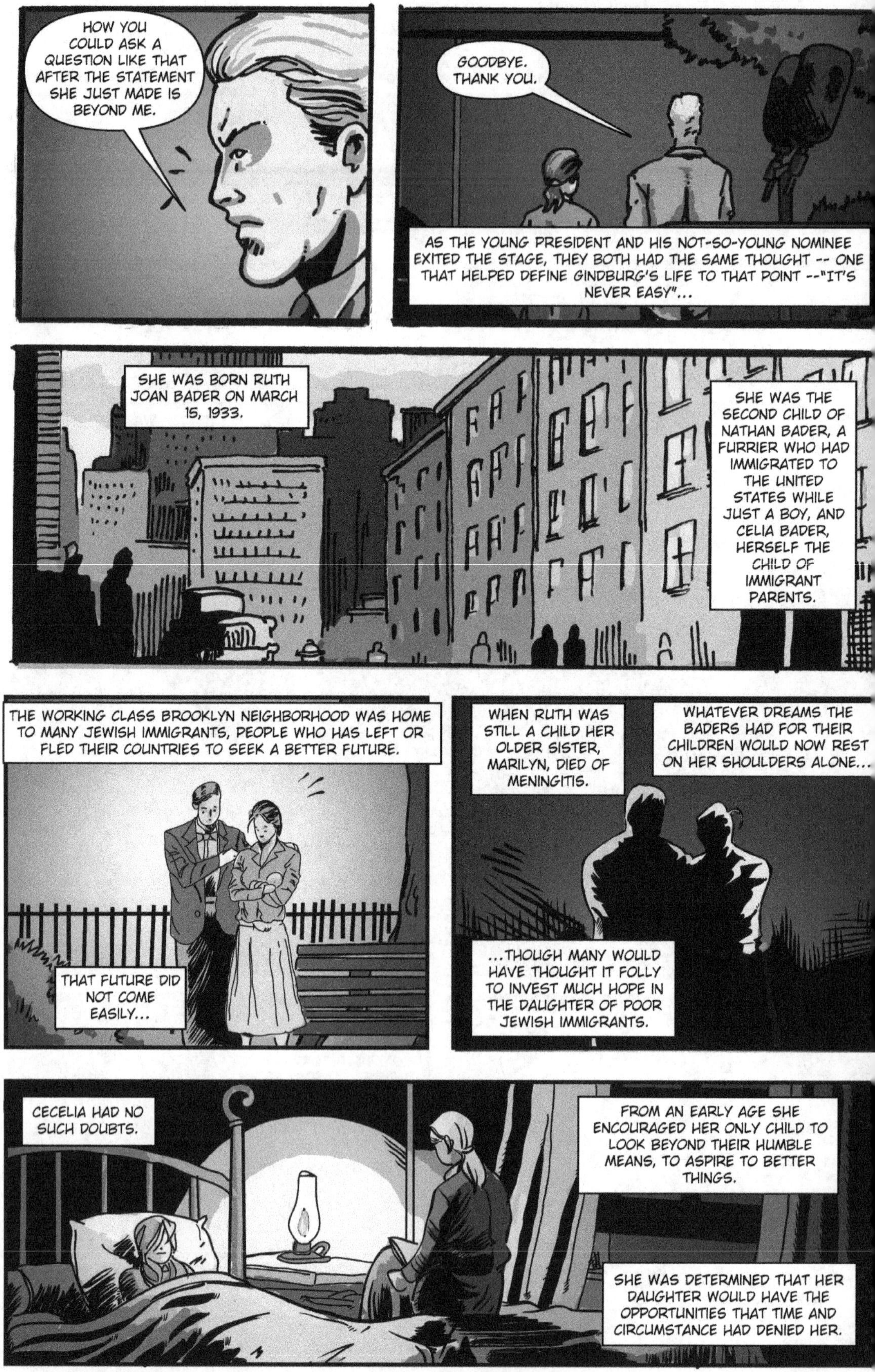
HOW YOU COULD ASK A QUESTION LIKE THAT AFTER THE STATEMENT SHE JUST MADE IS BEYOND ME.
GOODBYE. THANK YOU.
AS THE YOUNG PRESIDENT AND HIS NOT-SO-YOUNG NOMINEE EXITED THE STAGE, THEY BOTH HAD THE SAME THOUGHT -- ONE THAT HELPED DEFINE GINDBURG'S LIFE TO THAT POINT --"IT'S NEVER EASY"...
SHE WAS BORN RUTH JOAN BADER ON MARCH 15, 1933.
SHE WAS THE SECOND CHILD OF NATHAN BADER, A FURRIER WHO HAD IMMIGRATED TO THE UNITED STATES WHILE JUST A BOY, AND CELIA BADER, HERSELF THE CHILD OF IMMIGRANT PARENTS.
THE WORKING CLASS BROOKLYN NEIGHBORHOOD WAS HOME TO MANY JEWISH IMMIGRANTS, PEOPLE WHO HAS LEFT OR FLED THEIR COUNTRIES TO SEEK A BETTER FUTURE.
THAT FUTURE DID NOT COME EASILY...
WHEN RUTH WAS STILL A CHILD HER OLDER SISTER, MARILYN, DIED OF MENINGITIS.
WHATEVER DREAMS THE BADERS HAD FOR THEIR CHILDREN WOULD NOW REST ON HER SHOULDERS ALONE...
...THOUGH MANY WOULD HAVE THOUGHT IT FOLLY TO INVEST MUCH HOPE IN THE DAUGHTER OF POOR JEWISH IMMIGRANTS.
CECELIA HAD NO SUCH DOUBTS.
FROM AN EARLY AGE SHE ENCOURAGED HER ONLY CHILD TO LOOK BEYOND THEIR HUMBLE MEANS, TO ASPIRE TO BETTER THINGS.
SHE WAS DETERMINED THAT HER DAUGHTER WOULD HAVE THE OPPORTUNITIES THAT TIME AND CIRCUMSTANCE HAD DENIED HER.

IN ANOTHER TIME, A WOMAN OF CECELIA'S INTELLIGENCE AND PASSION FOR LEARNING WOULD HAVE ALMOST CERTAINLY GONE TO COLLEGE.

HOWEVER, FOR A FAMILY OF NEWLY ARRIVED IMMIGRANTS, SUCH OPPORTUNITIES WERE RARE.

SHE WENT TO WORK IN A GARMENT FACTORY TO HELP RAISE THE MONEY TO PUT HER BROTHER THROUGH SCHOOL.

IT WAS THE LOGICAL CHOICE.

EVEN AN EDUCATED WOMAN WOULD FIND FEW OPPORTUNITIES TO FIND THE KIND OF CAREER THAT COULD BE USED TO HELP HER FAMILY.

HER MOTHER'S ACT OF SELFLESSNESS WOULD NEVER BE FORGOTTEN BY HER DAUGHTER.

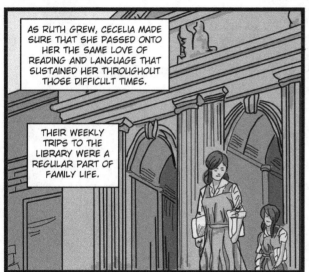

AS RUTH GREW, CECELIA MADE SURE THAT SHE PASSED ONTO HER THE SAME LOVE OF READING AND LANGUAGE THAT SUSTAINED HER THROUGHOUT THOSE DIFFICULT TIMES.

THEIR WEEKLY TRIPS TO THE LIBRARY WERE A REGULAR PART OF FAMILY LIFE.

AS WAS THEIR LOVE FOR THE RADIO SHOWS THAT FOUND HUMOR IN THE LIVES OF THE NATION'S GROWING IMMIGRANT POPULATION.

"THE RISE OF THE GOLDBERGS," A SITUATION COMEDY ABOUT A MIDDLE CLASS JEWISH FAMILY IN NEW YORK, WAS A FAVORITE.

MANY YEARS LATER, A SUPREME COURT JUSTICE WOULD ACCIDENTALLY REFER TO RUTH AS "MRS. GOLDBERG", A MISTAKE SHE FOUND DELIGHTFUL.

RUTH'S TALENTS BLOSSOMED ASS SHE ENTERED HIGH SCHOOL.

WHATEVER THE LIMITATIONS OF THE TIME, HER MOTHER LEFT NO DOUBT WHAT WAS TO BE EXPECTED OF HER.

CECELIA TOLD HER DAUGHTER TO STRIVE FOR TWO GOALS...

...ONE WAS TO BE A LADY.

THE OTHER WAS TO BE INDEPENDENT.

RUTH FULFILLED BOTH GOALS. SHE EXCELLED IN SCHOOL, FINISHING NEAR THE TOP OF HER CLASS IN ACADEMICS.

AT AN EARLY AGE SHE SHOWED A GIFT FOR WRITING AND AN INTEREST IN THE LAW.

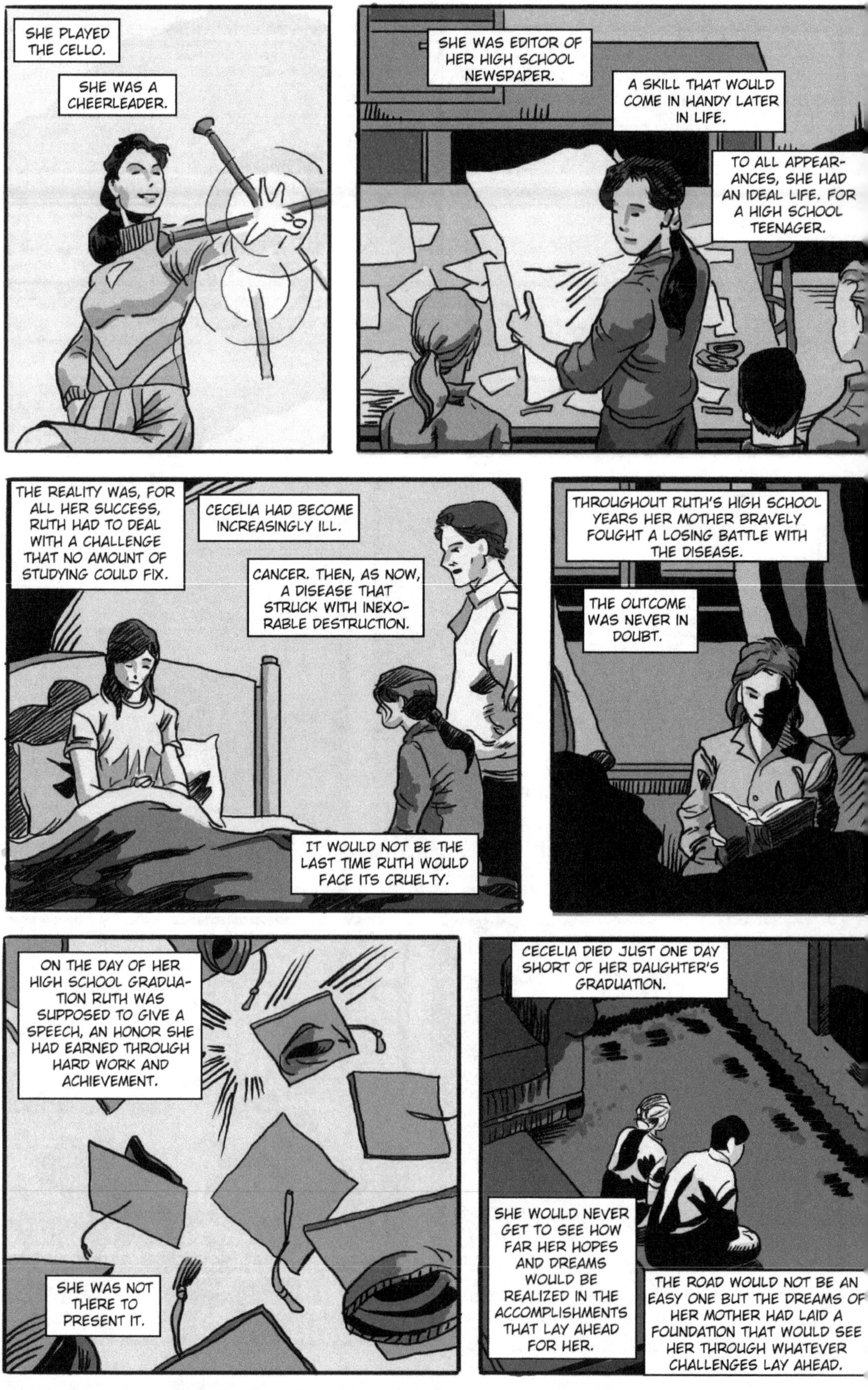
SHE PLAYED THE CELLO.
SHE WAS A CHEERLEADER.
SHE WAS EDITOR OF HER HIGH SCHOOL NEWSPAPER.
A SKILL THAT WOULD COME IN HANDY LATER IN LIFE.
TO ALL APPEARANCES, SHE HAD AN IDEAL LIFE. FOR A HIGH SCHOOL TEENAGER.
THE REALITY WAS, FOR ALL HER SUCCESS, RUTH HAD TO DEAL WITH A CHALLENGE THAT NO AMOUNT OF STUDYING COULD FIX.
CECELIA HAD BECOME INCREASINGLY ILL.
CANCER. THEN, AS NOW, A DISEASE THAT STRUCK WITH INEXORABLE DESTRUCTION.
IT WOULD NOT BE THE LAST TIME RUTH WOULD FACE ITS CRUELTY.
THROUGHOUT RUTH'S HIGH SCHOOL YEARS HER MOTHER BRAVELY FOUGHT A LOSING BATTLE WITH THE DISEASE.
THE OUTCOME WAS NEVER IN DOUBT.
ON THE DAY OF HER HIGH SCHOOL GRADUATION RUTH WAS SUPPOSED TO GIVE A SPEECH, AN HONOR SHE HAD EARNED THROUGH HARD WORK AND ACHIEVEMENT.
SHE WAS NOT THERE TO PRESENT IT.
CECELIA DIED JUST ONE DAY SHORT OF HER DAUGHTER'S GRADUATION.
SHE WOULD NEVER GET TO SEE HOW FAR HER HOPES AND DREAMS WOULD BE REALIZED IN THE ACCOMPLISHMENTS THAT LAY AHEAD FOR HER.
THE ROAD WOULD NOT BE AN EASY ONE BUT THE DREAMS OF HER MOTHER HAD LAID A FOUNDATION THAT WOULD SEE HER THROUGH WHATEVER CHALLENGES LAY AHEAD.

THE LOSS OF HER BELOVED MOTHER WEIGHED HEAVILY ON HER AS SHE WENT TO THE PRESTIGIOUS CORNEL COLLEGE, BUT RUTH ROSE TO THE CHALLENGE WITH TYPICAL EXCELLENCE.

SHE WAS FIRST IN HER CLASS

AND SHE MET THE LOVE OF HER LIFE.

MARTIN D. GINSBURG, A FELLOW LAW STUDENT, IMPRESSED HER WITH HIS EASY HUMOR AND KEEN INTELLIGENCE.

THEY MET ON A BLIND DATE.

IT WAS THE BEGINNING OF A 56 YEAR PARTNERSHIP THAT WOULD TAKE THEM THROUGH GOOD TIMES AND BAD.

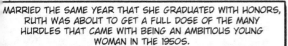

MARRIED THE SAME YEAR THAT SHE GRADUATED WITH HONORS, RUTH WAS ABOUT TO GET A FULL DOSE OF THE MANY HURDLES THAT CAME WITH BEING AN AMBITIOUS YOUNG WOMAN IN THE 1950S.

IN 1954 MARTIN WAS DRAFTED TO SERVE IN THE ARMY. THEIR FIRST DAUGHTER, JANE, WAS BORN SHORTLY AFTERWARD.

AMBITION WAS PUT ON HOLD AS FAMILY AND COUNTRY DEMANDED FULL ATTENTION.

BUT NEITHER OF THEM WAS ABOUT TO LET THEIR POTENTIAL GO TO WASTE.

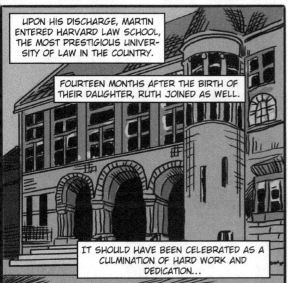

UPON HIS DISCHARGE, MARTIN ENTERED HARVARD LAW SCHOOL, THE MOST PRESTIGIOUS UNIVERSITY OF LAW IN THE COUNTRY.

FOURTEEN MONTHS AFTER THE BIRTH OF THEIR DAUGHTER, RUTH JOINED AS WELL.

IT SHOULD HAVE BEEN CELEBRATED AS A CULMINATION OF HARD WORK AND DEDICATION...

...BUT IT'S NEVER EASY...

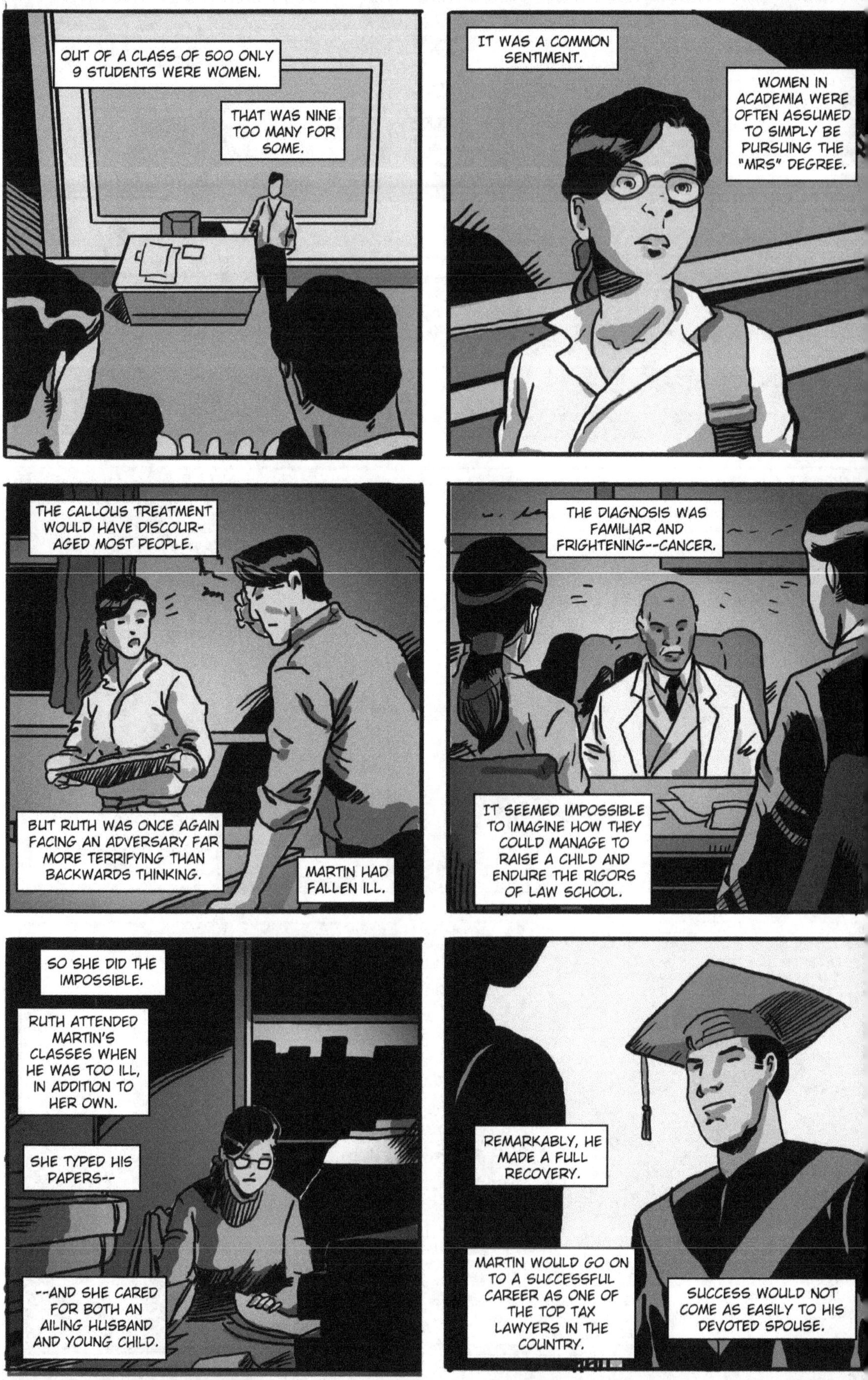
OUT OF A CLASS OF 500 ONLY 9 STUDENTS WERE WOMEN.
THAT WAS NINE TOO MANY FOR SOME.
IT WAS A COMMON SENTIMENT.
WOMEN IN ACADEMIA WERE OFTEN ASSUMED TO SIMPLY BE PURSUING THE "MRS" DEGREE.
THE CALLOUS TREATMENT WOULD HAVE DISCOURAGED MOST PEOPLE.
BUT RUTH WAS ONCE AGAIN FACING AN ADVERSARY FAR MORE TERRIFYING THAN BACKWARDS THINKING.
MARTIN HAD FALLEN ILL.
THE DIAGNOSIS WAS FAMILIAR AND FRIGHTENING--CANCER.
IT SEEMED IMPOSSIBLE TO IMAGINE HOW THEY COULD MANAGE TO RAISE A CHILD AND ENDURE THE RIGORS OF LAW SCHOOL.
SO SHE DID THE IMPOSSIBLE.
RUTH ATTENDED MARTIN'S CLASSES WHEN HE WAS TOO ILL, IN ADDITION TO HER OWN.
SHE TYPED HIS PAPERS--
--AND SHE CARED FOR BOTH AN AILING HUSBAND AND YOUNG CHILD.
REMARKABLY, HE MADE A FULL RECOVERY.
MARTIN WOULD GO ON TO A SUCCESSFUL CAREER AS ONE OF THE TOP TAX LAWYERS IN THE COUNTRY.
SUCCESS WOULD NOT COME AS EASILY TO HIS DEVOTED SPOUSE.

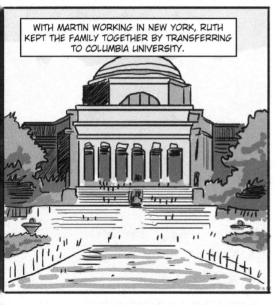

WITH MARTIN WORKING IN NEW YORK, RUTH KEPT THE FAMILY TOGETHER BY TRANSFERRING TO COLUMBIA UNIVERSITY.

SHE BECAME THE FIRST LAW STUDENT--MALE OR FEMALE--TO MAKE THE LAW REVIEW AT BOTH HARVARD AND COLUMBIA.

WHILE THE VENUE HAD CHANGED, HER RECORD OF SUCCESS HAD NOT.

SHE GRADUATED TIED FOR FIRST IN HER CLASS.

SUCCESS SEEMED ALL BUT ASSURED.

REALITY CAME AS A SHOCK.

EVEN YEARS LATER THE REJECTIONS STUNG.

NO ONE WILL HIRE ME BECAUSE I'M A WOMAN, A MOTHER AND A JEW.

SHE HAD MANY DEFENDERS. ONE OF HER HARVARD PROFESSORS RECOMMENDED HER FOR A CLERKSHIP ON THE SUPREME COURT.

JUSTICE FELIX FRANK-FURTER REPLIED THAT HE WAS NOT READY TO HIRE A WOMAN...

AFTER 12 INTERVIEWS AT LAW FIRMS RESULTED IN ONLY 2 EVEN BOTHERING WITH A FOLLOW-UP. NONE WOULD HIRE HER.

SUCCESS, SO VALIANTLY FOUGHT FOR, SEEMED FURTHER AWAY THAN EVER.

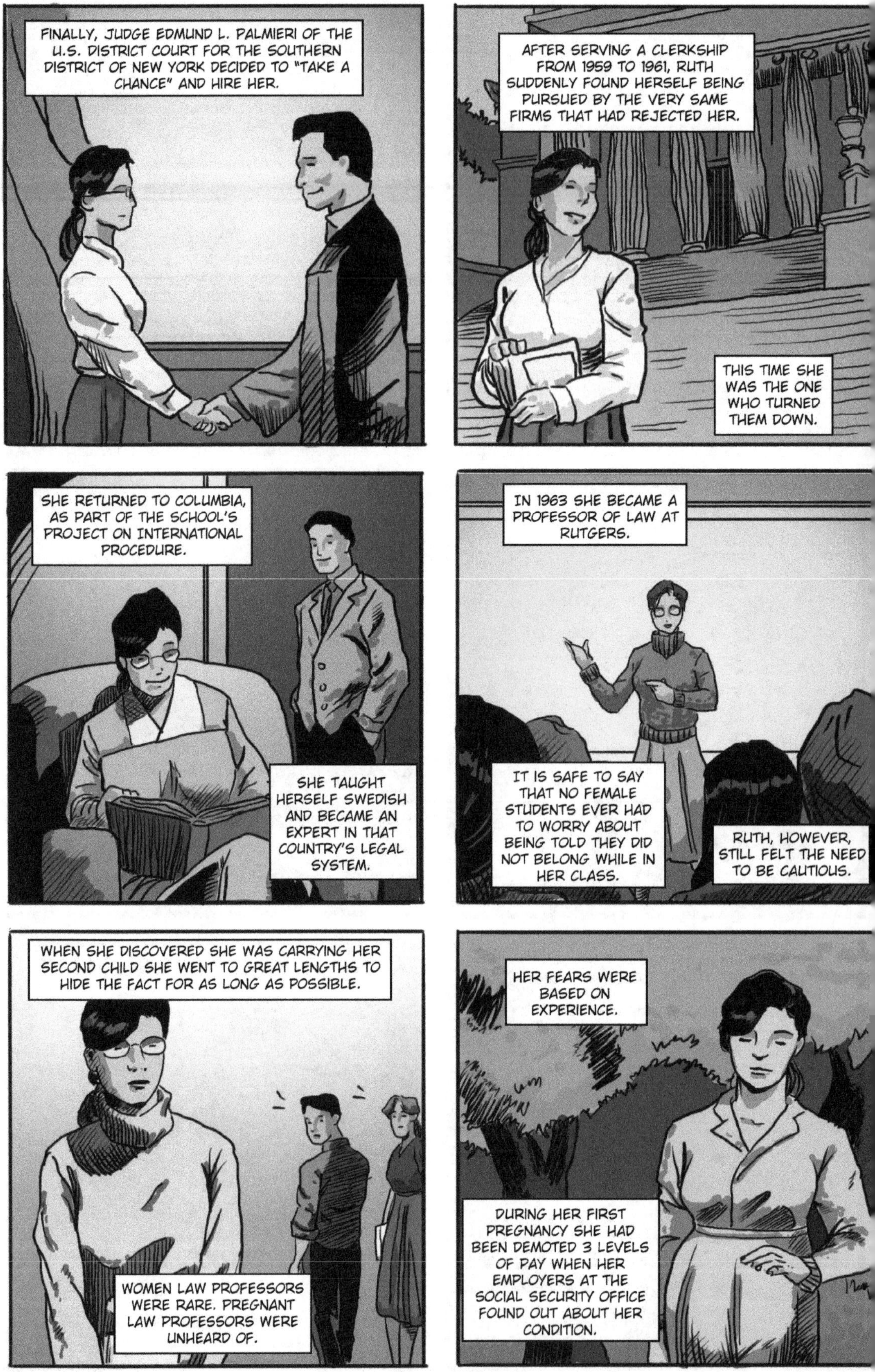
FINALLY, JUDGE EDMUND L. PALMIERI OF THE U.S. DISTRICT COURT FOR THE SOUTHERN DISTRICT OF NEW YORK DECIDED TO "TAKE A CHANCE" AND HIRE HER.
AFTER SERVING A CLERKSHIP FROM 1959 TO 1961, RUTH SUDDENLY FOUND HERSELF BEING PURSUED BY THE VERY SAME FIRMS THAT HAD REJECTED HER.
THIS TIME SHE WAS THE ONE WHO TURNED THEM DOWN.
SHE RETURNED TO COLUMBIA, AS PART OF THE SCHOOL'S PROJECT ON INTERNATIONAL PROCEDURE.
SHE TAUGHT HERSELF SWEDISH AND BECAME AN EXPERT IN THAT COUNTRY'S LEGAL SYSTEM.
IN 1963 SHE BECAME A PROFESSOR OF LAW AT RUTGERS.
IT IS SAFE TO SAY THAT NO FEMALE STUDENTS EVER HAD TO WORRY ABOUT BEING TOLD THEY DID NOT BELONG WHILE IN HER CLASS.
RUTH, HOWEVER, STILL FELT THE NEED TO BE CAUTIOUS.
WHEN SHE DISCOVERED SHE WAS CARRYING HER SECOND CHILD SHE WENT TO GREAT LENGTHS TO HIDE THE FACT FOR AS LONG AS POSSIBLE.
WOMEN LAW PROFESSORS WERE RARE. PREGNANT LAW PROFESSORS WERE UNHEARD OF.
HER FEARS WERE BASED ON EXPERIENCE.
DURING HER FIRST PREGNANCY SHE HAD BEEN DEMOTED 3 LEVELS OF PAY WHEN HER EMPLOYERS AT THE SOCIAL SECURITY OFFICE FOUND OUT ABOUT HER CONDITION.

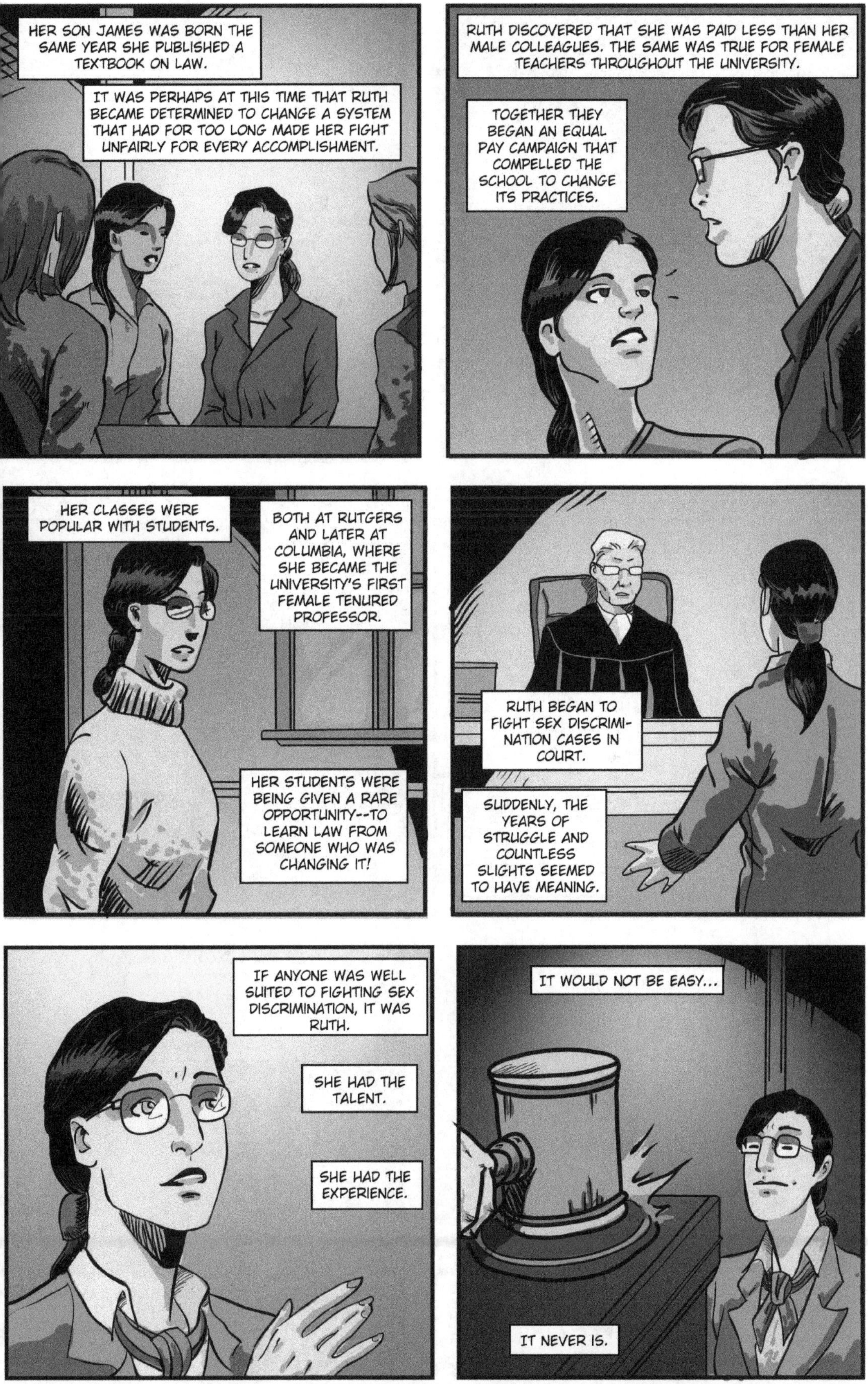
HER SON JAMES WAS BORN THE SAME YEAR SHE PUBLISHED A TEXTBOOK ON LAW.
IT WAS PERHAPS AT THIS TIME THAT RUTH BECAME DETERMINED TO CHANGE A SYSTEM THAT HAD FOR TOO LONG MADE HER FIGHT UNFAIRLY FOR EVERY ACCOMPLISHMENT.
RUTH DISCOVERED THAT SHE WAS PAID LESS THAN HER MALE COLLEAGUES. THE SAME WAS TRUE FOR FEMALE TEACHERS THROUGHOUT THE UNIVERSITY.
TOGETHER THEY BEGAN AN EQUAL PAY CAMPAIGN THAT COMPELLED THE SCHOOL TO CHANGE ITS PRACTICES.
HER CLASSES WERE POPULAR WITH STUDENTS.
BOTH AT RUTGERS AND LATER AT COLUMBIA, WHERE SHE BECAME THE UNIVERSITY'S FIRST FEMALE TENURED PROFESSOR.
HER STUDENTS WERE BEING GIVEN A RARE OPPORTUNITY--TO LEARN LAW FROM SOMEONE WHO WAS CHANGING IT!
RUTH BEGAN TO FIGHT SEX DISCRIMINATION CASES IN COURT.
SUDDENLY, THE YEARS OF STRUGGLE AND COUNTLESS SLIGHTS SEEMED TO HAVE MEANING.
IF ANYONE WAS WELL SUITED TO FIGHTING SEX DISCRIMINATION, IT WAS RUTH.
SHE HAD THE TALENT.
SHE HAD THE EXPERIENCE.
IT WOULD NOT BE EASY...
IT NEVER IS.

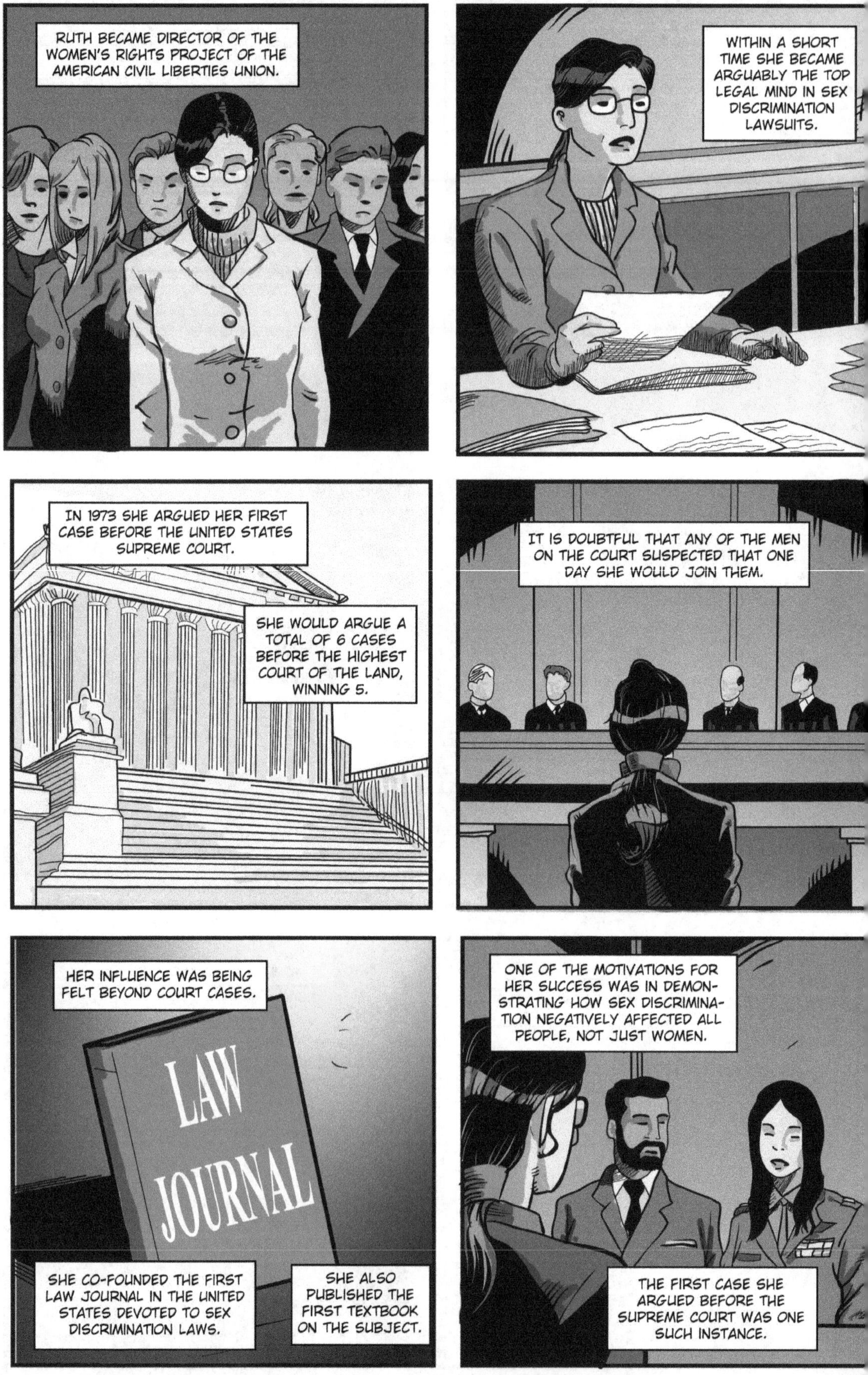
RUTH BECAME DIRECTOR OF THE WOMEN'S RIGHTS PROJECT OF THE AMERICAN CIVIL LIBERTIES UNION.
WITHIN A SHORT TIME SHE BECAME ARGUABLY THE TOP LEGAL MIND IN SEX DISCRIMINATION LAWSUITS.
IN 1973 SHE ARGUED HER FIRST CASE BEFORE THE UNITED STATES SUPREME COURT.
SHE WOULD ARGUE A TOTAL OF 6 CASES BEFORE THE HIGHEST COURT OF THE LAND, WINNING 5.
IT IS DOUBTFUL THAT ANY OF THE MEN ON THE COURT SUSPECTED THAT ONE DAY SHE WOULD JOIN THEM.
HER INFLUENCE WAS BEING FELT BEYOND COURT CASES.
LAW JOURNAL
SHE CO-FOUNDED THE FIRST LAW JOURNAL IN THE UNITED STATES DEVOTED TO SEX DISCRIMINATION LAWS.
SHE ALSO PUBLISHED THE FIRST TEXTBOOK ON THE SUBJECT.
ONE OF THE MOTIVATIONS FOR HER SUCCESS WAS IN DEMONSTRATING HOW SEX DISCRIMINATION NEGATIVELY AFFECTED ALL PEOPLE, NOT JUST WOMEN.
THE FIRST CASE SHE ARGUED BEFORE THE SUPREME COURT WAS ONE SUCH INSTANCE.

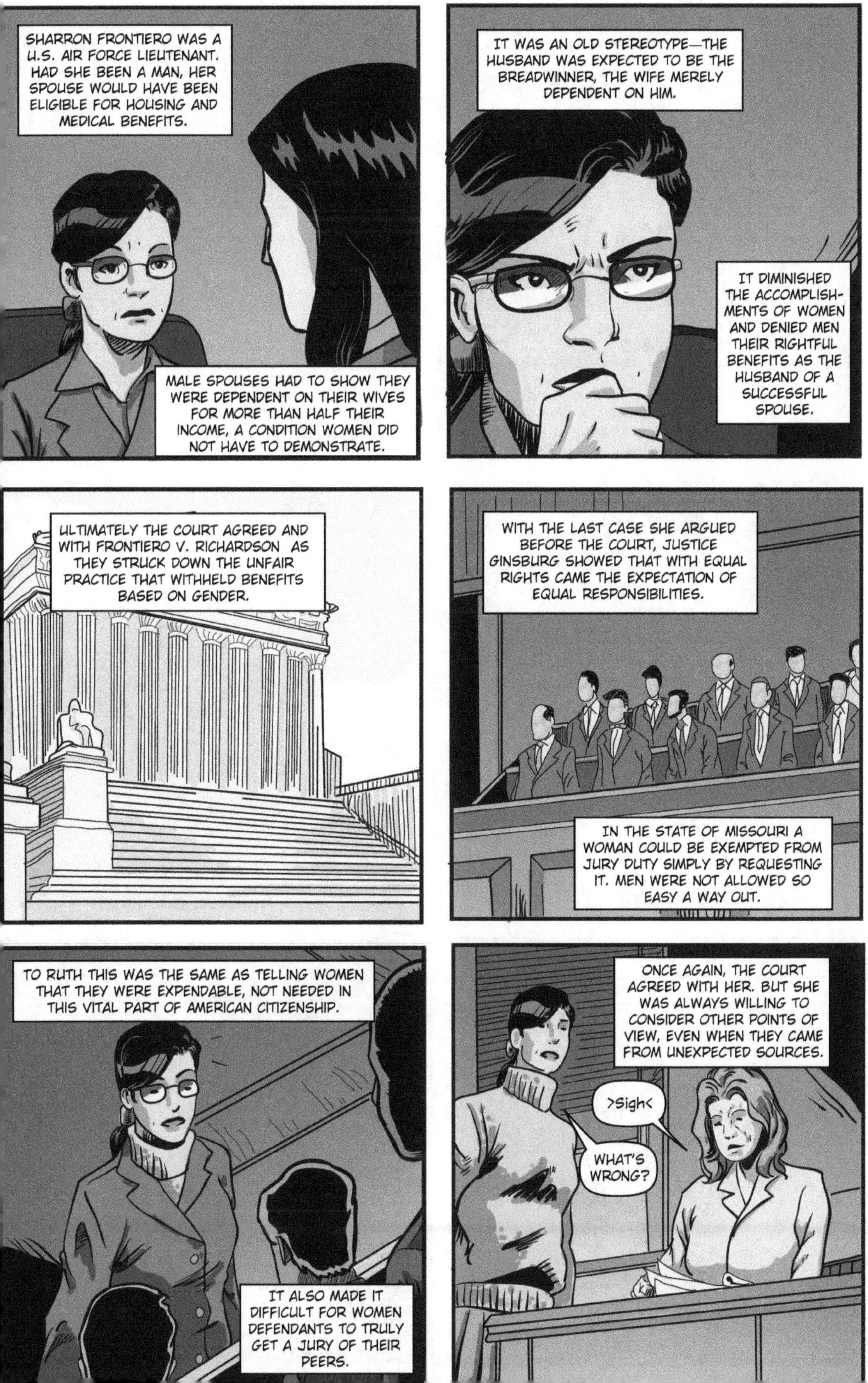
SHARRON FRONTIERO WAS A U.S. AIR FORCE LIEUTENANT. HAD SHE BEEN A MAN, HER SPOUSE WOULD HAVE BEEN ELIGIBLE FOR HOUSING AND MEDICAL BENEFITS.
MALE SPOUSES HAD TO SHOW THEY WERE DEPENDENT ON THEIR WIVES FOR MORE THAN HALF THEIR INCOME, A CONDITION WOMEN DID NOT HAVE TO DEMONSTRATE.
IT WAS AN OLD STEREOTYPE—THE HUSBAND WAS EXPECTED TO BE THE BREADWINNER, THE WIFE MERELY DEPENDENT ON HIM.
IT DIMINISHED THE ACCOMPLISHMENTS OF WOMEN AND DENIED MEN THEIR RIGHTFUL BENEFITS AS THE HUSBAND OF A SUCCESSFUL SPOUSE.
ULTIMATELY THE COURT AGREED AND WITH FRONTIERO V. RICHARDSON AS THEY STRUCK DOWN THE UNFAIR PRACTICE THAT WITHHELD BENEFITS BASED ON GENDER.
WITH THE LAST CASE SHE ARGUED BEFORE THE COURT, JUSTICE GINSBURG SHOWED THAT WITH EQUAL RIGHTS CAME THE EXPECTATION OF EQUAL RESPONSIBILITIES.
IN THE STATE OF MISSOURI A WOMAN COULD BE EXEMPTED FROM JURY DUTY SIMPLY BY REQUESTING IT. MEN WERE NOT ALLOWED SO EASY A WAY OUT.
TO RUTH THIS WAS THE SAME AS TELLING WOMEN THAT THEY WERE EXPENDABLE, NOT NEEDED IN THIS VITAL PART OF AMERICAN CITIZENSHIP.
IT ALSO MADE IT DIFFICULT FOR WOMEN DEFENDANTS TO TRULY GET A JURY OF THEIR PEERS.
ONCE AGAIN, THE COURT AGREED WITH HER. BUT SHE WAS ALWAYS WILLING TO CONSIDER OTHER POINTS OF VIEW, EVEN WHEN THEY CAME FROM UNEXPECTED SOURCES.
>Sigh<
WHAT'S WRONG?

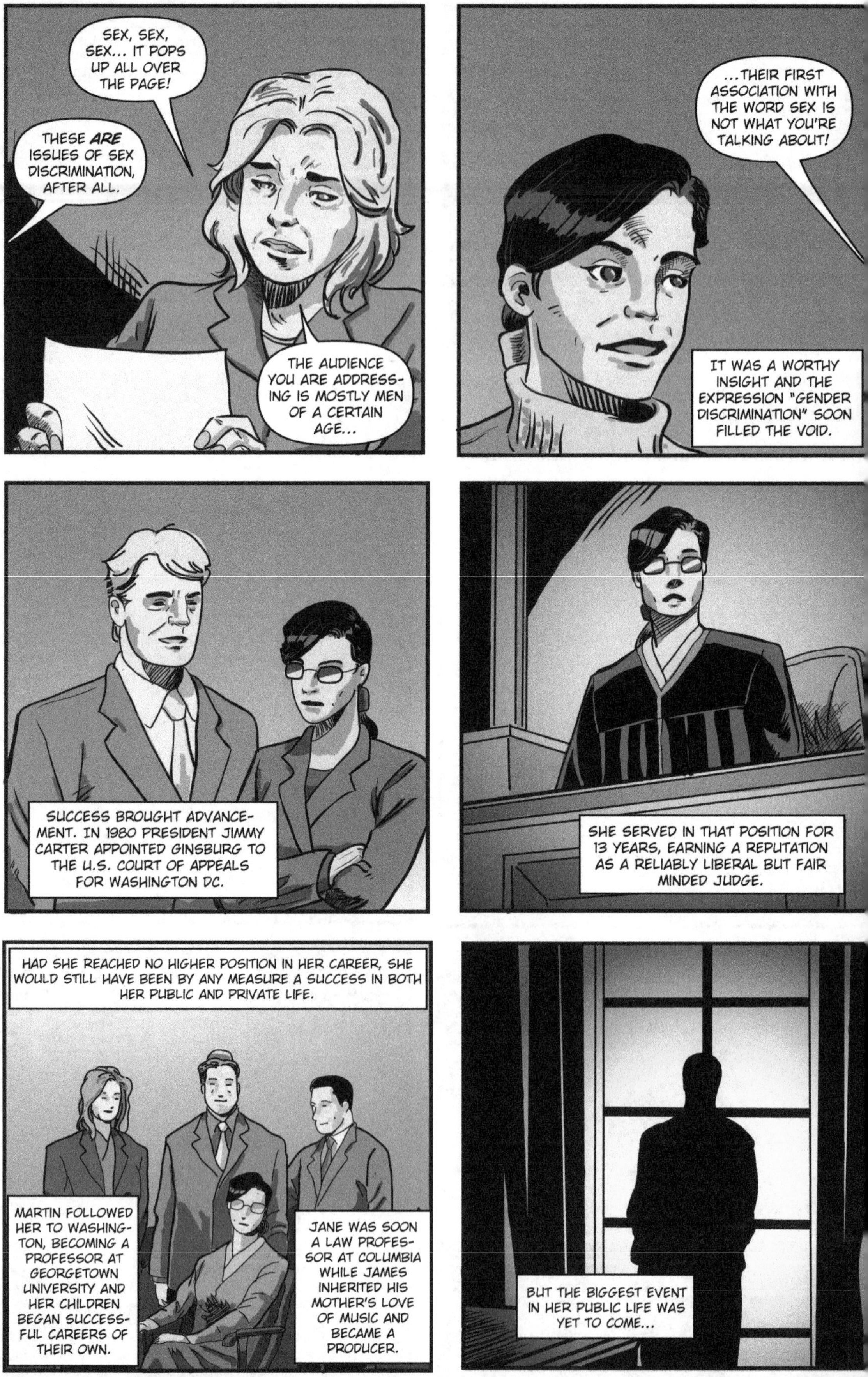

SEX, SEX, SEX... IT POPS UP ALL OVER THE PAGE!
THESE ARE ISSUES OF SEX DISCRIMINATION, AFTER ALL.
THE AUDIENCE YOU ARE ADDRESSING IS MOSTLY MEN OF A CERTAIN AGE...
...THEIR FIRST ASSOCIATION WITH THE WORD SEX IS NOT WHAT YOU'RE TALKING ABOUT!
IT WAS A WORTHY INSIGHT AND THE EXPRESSION "GENDER DISCRIMINATION" SOON FILLED THE VOID.
SUCCESS BROUGHT ADVANCEMENT. IN 1980 PRESIDENT JIMMY CARTER APPOINTED GINSBURG TO THE U.S. COURT OF APPEALS FOR WASHINGTON DC.
SHE SERVED IN THAT POSITION FOR 13 YEARS, EARNING A REPUTATION AS A RELIABLY LIBERAL BUT FAIR MINDED JUDGE.
HAD SHE REACHED NO HIGHER POSITION IN HER CAREER, SHE WOULD STILL HAVE BEEN BY ANY MEASURE A SUCCESS IN BOTH HER PUBLIC AND PRIVATE LIFE.
MARTIN FOLLOWED HER TO WASHINGTON, BECOMING A PROFESSOR AT GEORGETOWN UNIVERSITY AND HER CHILDREN BEGAN SUCCESSFUL CAREERS OF THEIR OWN.
JANE WAS SOON A LAW PROFESSOR AT COLUMBIA WHILE JAMES INHERITED HIS MOTHER'S LOVE OF MUSIC AND BECAME A PRODUCER.
BUT THE BIGGEST EVENT IN HER PUBLIC LIFE WAS YET TO COME...

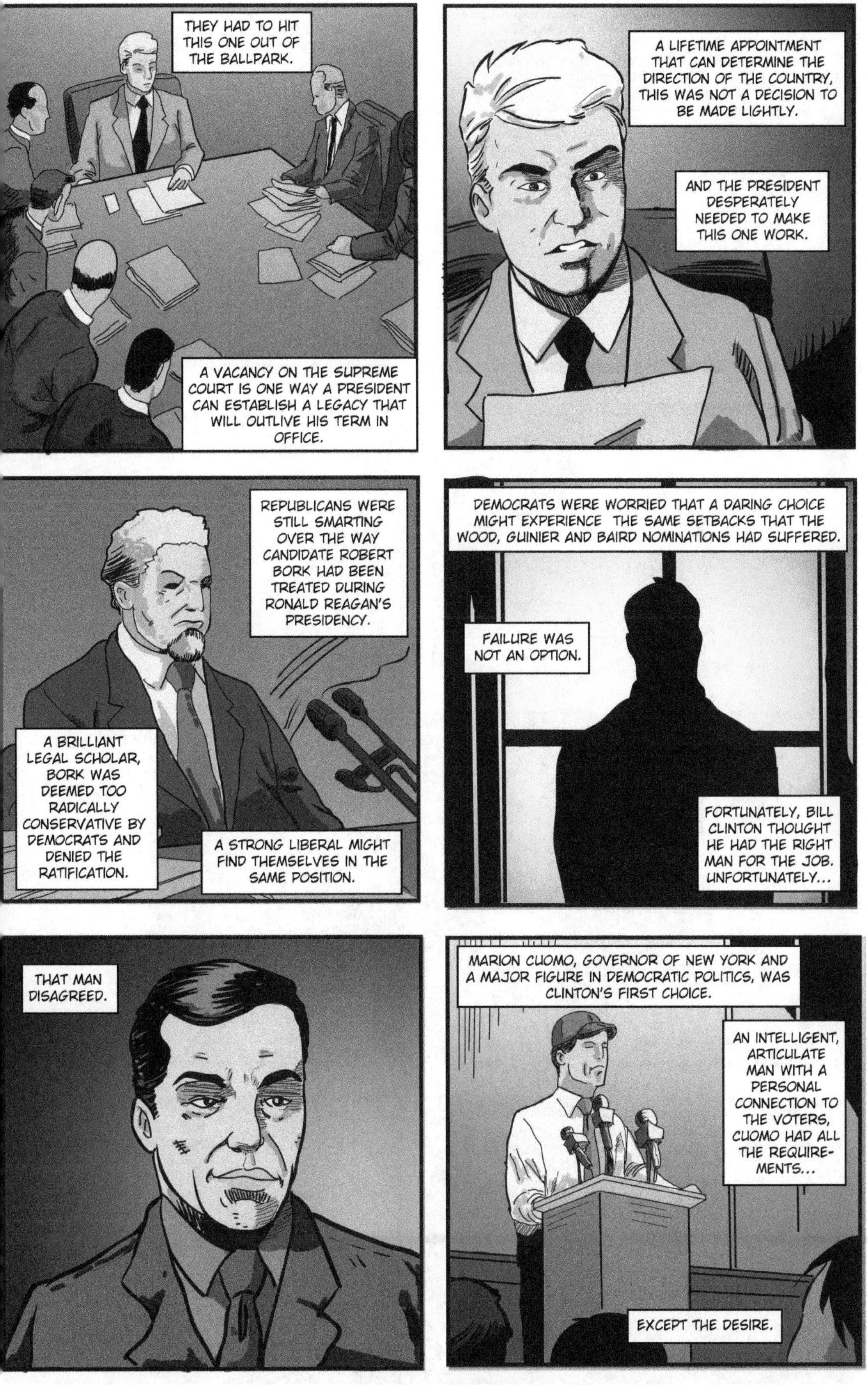
THEY HAD TO HIT THIS ONE OUT OF THE BALLPARK.
A VACANCY ON THE SUPREME COURT IS ONE WAY A PRESIDENT CAN ESTABLISH A LEGACY THAT WILL OUTLIVE HIS TERM IN OFFICE.
A LIFETIME APPOINTMENT THAT CAN DETERMINE THE DIRECTION OF THE COUNTRY, THIS WAS NOT A DECISION TO BE MADE LIGHTLY.
AND THE PRESIDENT DESPERATELY NEEDED TO MAKE THIS ONE WORK.
REPUBLICANS WERE STILL SMARTING OVER THE WAY CANDIDATE ROBERT BORK HAD BEEN TREATED DURING RONALD REAGAN'S PRESIDENCY.
A BRILLIANT LEGAL SCHOLAR, BORK WAS DEEMED TOO RADICALLY CONSERVATIVE BY DEMOCRATS AND DENIED THE RATIFICATION.
A STRONG LIBERAL MIGHT FIND THEMSELVES IN THE SAME POSITION.
DEMOCRATS WERE WORRIED THAT A DARING CHOICE MIGHT EXPERIENCE THE SAME SETBACKS THAT THE WOOD, GUINIER AND BAIRD NOMINATIONS HAD SUFFERED.
FAILURE WAS NOT AN OPTION.
FORTUNATELY, BILL CLINTON THOUGHT HE HAD THE RIGHT MAN FOR THE JOB. UNFORTUNATELY...
THAT MAN DISAGREED.
MARION CUOMO, GOVERNOR OF NEW YORK AND A MAJOR FIGURE IN DEMOCRATIC POLITICS, WAS CLINTON'S FIRST CHOICE.
AN INTELLIGENT, ARTICULATE MAN WITH A PERSONAL CONNECTION TO THE VOTERS, CUOMO HAD ALL THE REQUIRE-MENTS...
EXCEPT THE DESIRE.

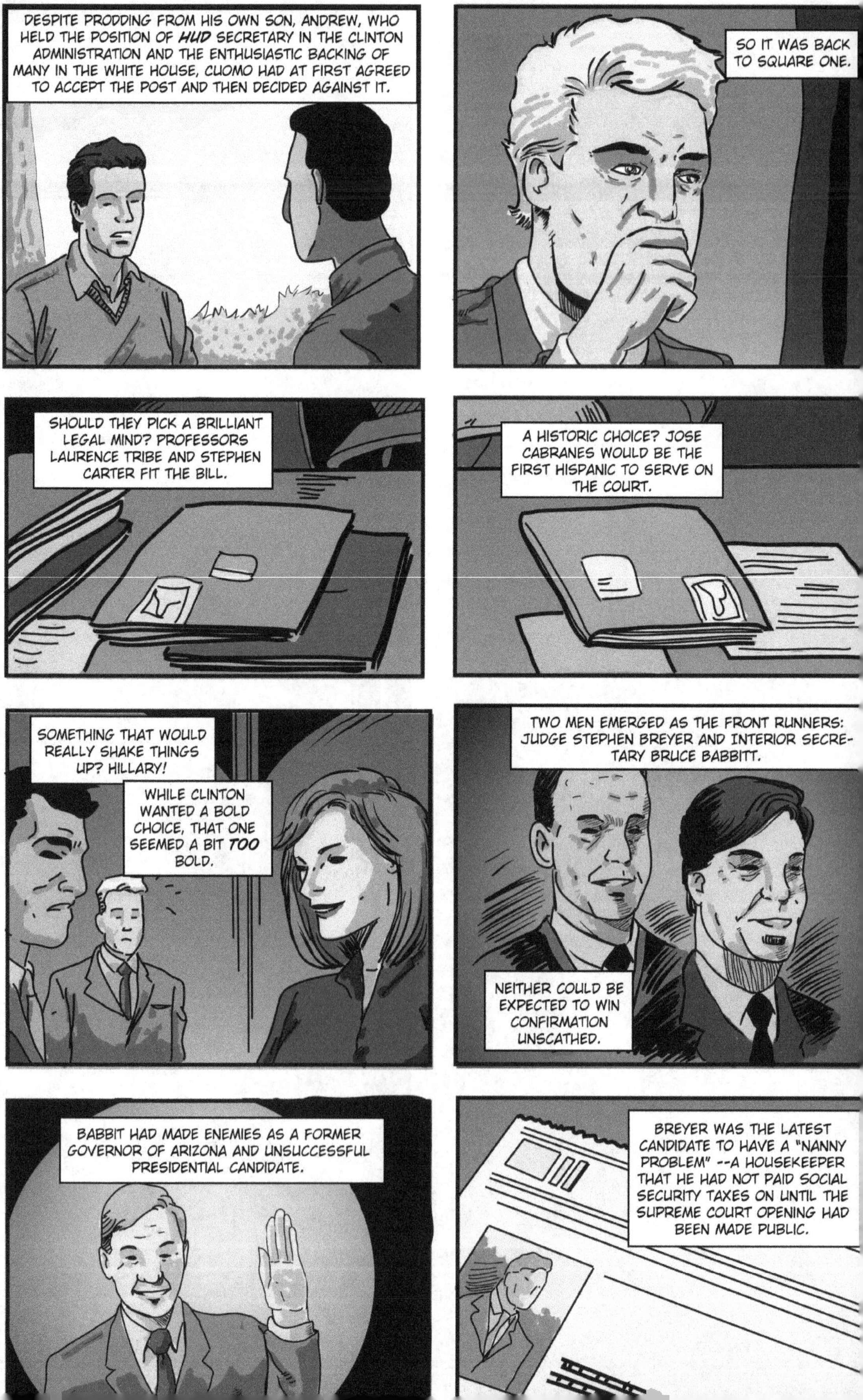
DESPITE PRODDING FROM HIS OWN SON, ANDREW, WHO HELD THE POSITION OF *HUD* SECRETARY IN THE CLINTON ADMINISTRATION AND THE ENTHUSIASTIC BACKING OF MANY IN THE WHITE HOUSE, CUOMO HAD AT FIRST AGREED TO ACCEPT THE POST AND THEN DECIDED AGAINST IT.
SO IT WAS BACK TO SQUARE ONE.
SHOULD THEY PICK A BRILLIANT LEGAL MIND? PROFESSORS LAURENCE TRIBE AND STEPHEN CARTER FIT THE BILL.
A HISTORIC CHOICE? JOSE CABRANES WOULD BE THE FIRST HISPANIC TO SERVE ON THE COURT.
SOMETHING THAT WOULD REALLY SHAKE THINGS UP? HILLARY!
WHILE CLINTON WANTED A BOLD CHOICE, THAT ONE SEEMED A BIT *TOO* BOLD.
TWO MEN EMERGED AS THE FRONT RUNNERS: JUDGE STEPHEN BREYER AND INTERIOR SECRETARY BRUCE BABBITT.
NEITHER COULD BE EXPECTED TO WIN CONFIRMATION UNSCATHED.
BABBIT HAD MADE ENEMIES AS A FORMER GOVERNOR OF ARIZONA AND UNSUCCESSFUL PRESIDENTIAL CANDIDATE.
BREYER WAS THE LATEST CANDIDATE TO HAVE A "NANNY PROBLEM" --A HOUSEKEEPER THAT HE HAD NOT PAID SOCIAL SECURITY TAXES ON UNTIL THE SUPREME COURT OPENING HAD BEEN MADE PUBLIC.

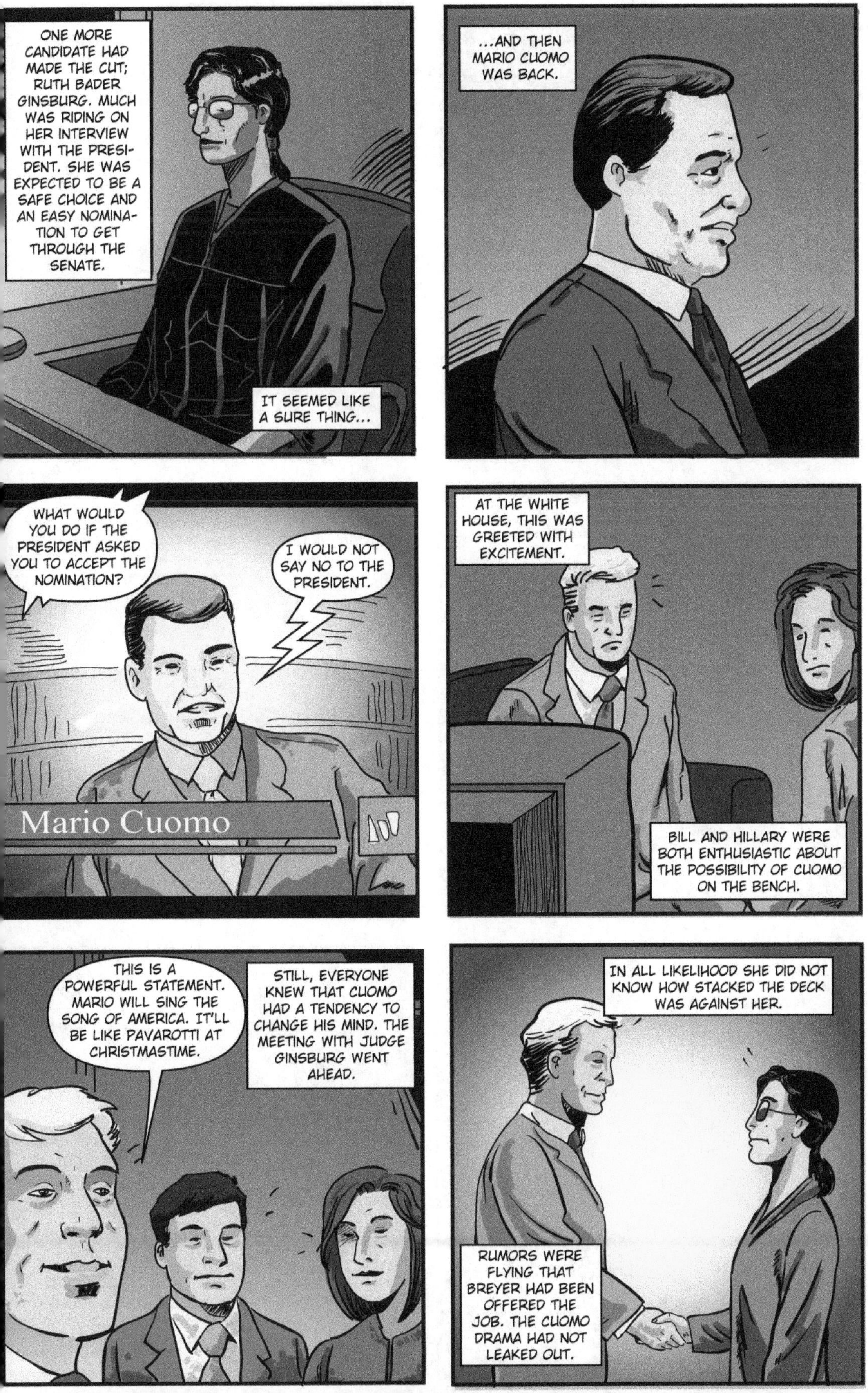
ONE MORE CANDIDATE HAD MADE THE CUT; RUTH BADER GINSBURG. MUCH WAS RIDING ON HER INTERVIEW WITH THE PRESIDENT. SHE WAS EXPECTED TO BE A SAFE CHOICE AND AN EASY NOMINATION TO GET THROUGH THE SENATE.
IT SEEMED LIKE A SURE THING...
...AND THEN MARIO CUOMO WAS BACK.
WHAT WOULD YOU DO IF THE PRESIDENT ASKED YOU TO ACCEPT THE NOMINATION?
I WOULD NOT SAY NO TO THE PRESIDENT.
Mario Cuomo
AT THE WHITE HOUSE, THIS WAS GREETED WITH EXCITEMENT.
BILL AND HILLARY WERE BOTH ENTHUSIASTIC ABOUT THE POSSIBILITY OF CUOMO ON THE BENCH.
THIS IS A POWERFUL STATEMENT. MARIO WILL SING THE SONG OF AMERICA. IT'LL BE LIKE PAVAROTTI AT CHRISTMASTIME.
STILL, EVERYONE KNEW THAT CUOMO HAD A TENDENCY TO CHANGE HIS MIND. THE MEETING WITH JUDGE GINSBURG WENT AHEAD.
IN ALL LIKELIHOOD SHE DID NOT KNOW HOW STACKED THE DECK WAS AGAINST HER.
RUMORS WERE FLYING THAT BREYER HAD BEEN OFFERED THE JOB. THE CUOMO DRAMA HAD NOT LEAKED OUT.

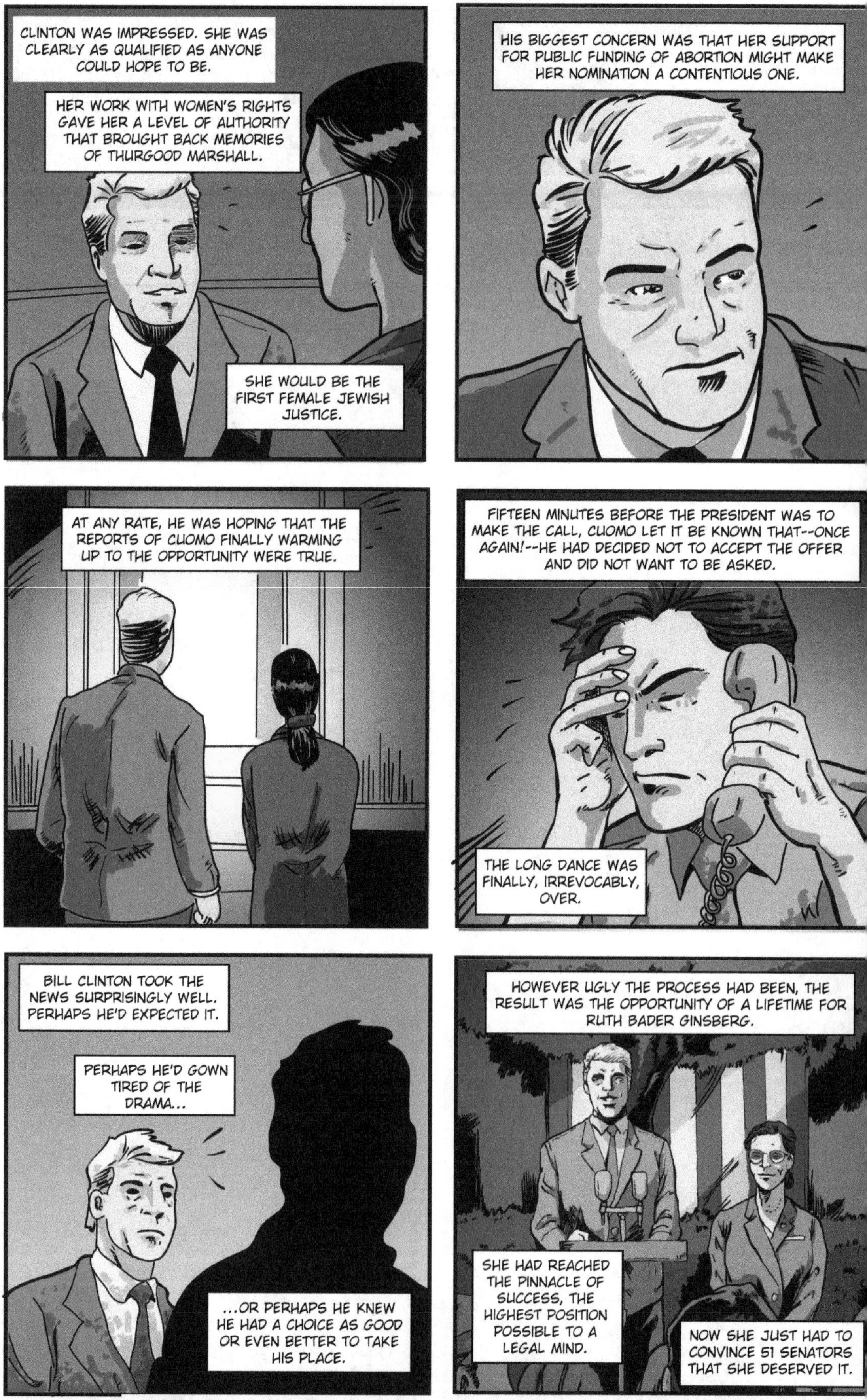
CLINTON WAS IMPRESSED. SHE WAS CLEARLY AS QUALIFIED AS ANYONE COULD HOPE TO BE.
HER WORK WITH WOMEN'S RIGHTS GAVE HER A LEVEL OF AUTHORITY THAT BROUGHT BACK MEMORIES OF THURGOOD MARSHALL.
SHE WOULD BE THE FIRST FEMALE JEWISH JUSTICE.
HIS BIGGEST CONCERN WAS THAT HER SUPPORT FOR PUBLIC FUNDING OF ABORTION MIGHT MAKE HER NOMINATION A CONTENTIOUS ONE.
AT ANY RATE, HE WAS HOPING THAT THE REPORTS OF CUOMO FINALLY WARMING UP TO THE OPPORTUNITY WERE TRUE.
FIFTEEN MINUTES BEFORE THE PRESIDENT WAS TO MAKE THE CALL, CUOMO LET IT BE KNOWN THAT--ONCE AGAIN!--HE HAD DECIDED NOT TO ACCEPT THE OFFER AND DID NOT WANT TO BE ASKED.
THE LONG DANCE WAS FINALLY, IRREVOCABLY, OVER.
BILL CLINTON TOOK THE NEWS SURPRISINGLY WELL. PERHAPS HE'D EXPECTED IT.
PERHAPS HE'D GOWN TIRED OF THE DRAMA...
...OR PERHAPS HE KNEW HE HAD A CHOICE AS GOOD OR EVEN BETTER TO TAKE HIS PLACE.
HOWEVER UGLY THE PROCESS HAD BEEN, THE RESULT WAS THE OPPORTUNITY OF A LIFETIME FOR RUTH BADER GINSBERG.
SHE HAD REACHED THE PINNACLE OF SUCCESS, THE HIGHEST POSITION POSSIBLE TO A LEGAL MIND.
NOW SHE JUST HAD TO CONVINCE 51 SENATORS THAT SHE DESERVED IT.

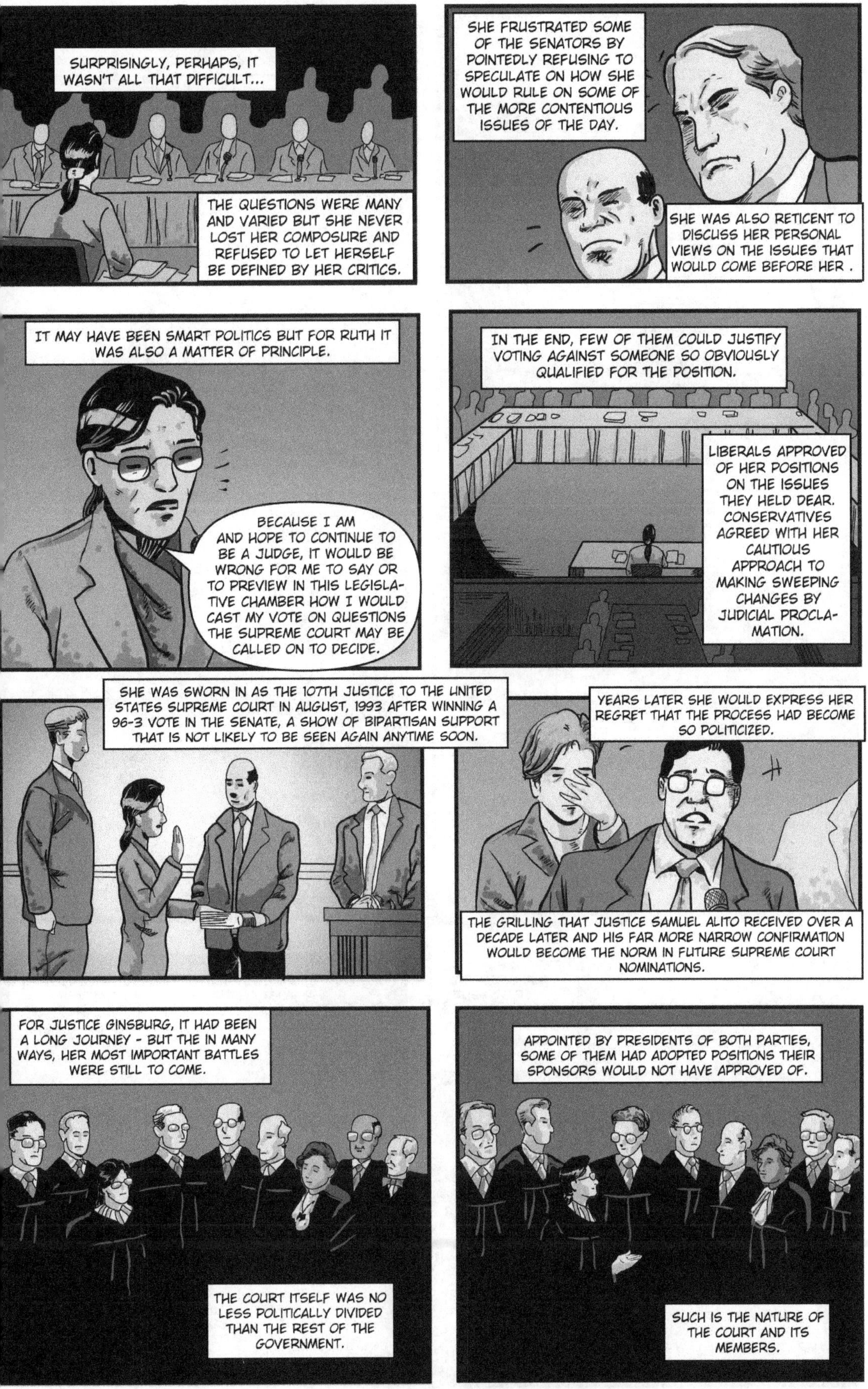
SURPRISINGLY, PERHAPS, IT WASN'T ALL THAT DIFFICULT...
THE QUESTIONS WERE MANY AND VARIED BUT SHE NEVER LOST HER COMPOSURE AND REFUSED TO LET HERSELF BE DEFINED BY HER CRITICS.
SHE FRUSTRATED SOME OF THE SENATORS BY POINTEDLY REFUSING TO SPECULATE ON HOW SHE WOULD RULE ON SOME OF THE MORE CONTENTIOUS ISSUES OF THE DAY.
SHE WAS ALSO RETICENT TO DISCUSS HER PERSONAL VIEWS ON THE ISSUES THAT WOULD COME BEFORE HER .
IT MAY HAVE BEEN SMART POLITICS BUT FOR RUTH IT WAS ALSO A MATTER OF PRINCIPLE.
BECAUSE I AM AND HOPE TO CONTINUE TO BE A JUDGE, IT WOULD BE WRONG FOR ME TO SAY OR TO PREVIEW IN THIS LEGISLATIVE CHAMBER HOW I WOULD CAST MY VOTE ON QUESTIONS THE SUPREME COURT MAY BE CALLED ON TO DECIDE.
IN THE END, FEW OF THEM COULD JUSTIFY VOTING AGAINST SOMEONE SO OBVIOUSLY QUALIFIED FOR THE POSITION.
LIBERALS APPROVED OF HER POSITIONS ON THE ISSUES THEY HELD DEAR. CONSERVATIVES AGREED WITH HER CAUTIOUS APPROACH TO MAKING SWEEPING CHANGES BY JUDICIAL PROCLAMATION.
SHE WAS SWORN IN AS THE 107TH JUSTICE TO THE UNITED STATES SUPREME COURT IN AUGUST, 1993 AFTER WINNING A 96-3 VOTE IN THE SENATE, A SHOW OF BIPARTISAN SUPPORT THAT IS NOT LIKELY TO BE SEEN AGAIN ANYTIME SOON.
YEARS LATER SHE WOULD EXPRESS HER REGRET THAT THE PROCESS HAD BECOME SO POLITICIZED.
THE GRILLING THAT JUSTICE SAMUEL ALITO RECEIVED OVER A DECADE LATER AND HIS FAR MORE NARROW CONFIRMATION WOULD BECOME THE NORM IN FUTURE SUPREME COURT NOMINATIONS.
FOR JUSTICE GINSBURG, IT HAD BEEN A LONG JOURNEY - BUT THE IN MANY WAYS, HER MOST IMPORTANT BATTLES WERE STILL TO COME.
THE COURT ITSELF WAS NO LESS POLITICALLY DIVIDED THAN THE REST OF THE GOVERNMENT.
APPOINTED BY PRESIDENTS OF BOTH PARTIES, SOME OF THEM HAD ADOPTED POSITIONS THEIR SPONSORS WOULD NOT HAVE APPROVED OF.
SUCH IS THE NATURE OF THE COURT AND ITS MEMBERS.

OF THE 9 MEMBERS, JUSTICE GINSBERG WOULD BE COUNTED AMONG THE 4 WHO WERE RELIABLE LIBERAL VOTES.

HARRY BLACKMUN, JOHN PAUL STEVENS, AND DAVID SOUTER WOULD OFTEN FIND THEMSELVES ON THE SAME SIDE OF AN OPINION.

ON THE CONSERVATIVE SIDE: CLARENCE THOMAS, ANTONIN SCALIA, SANDRA DAY O'CONNOR AND CHIEF JUSTICE WILLIAM REHNQUIST WERE USUALLY RELIABLE CONSERVATIVE VOTES

JUSTICE KENNEDY WAS OFTEN THE SWING VOTE IN CONTENTIOUS 5 TO 4 VOTES.

NEW MEMBERS HAVE COME IN AS OTHERS HAVE RETIRED BUT THIS POLITICAL SPLIT HAS REMAINED.

THROUGH ALL THE CHANGES, RUTH BADER GINSBURG NEVER WAVERED IN HER DEDICATION TO ADVANCING THE RIGHTS OF WOMEN.

ONE OF HER SIGNATURE DECISIONS WAS IN UNITED STATES VS VIRGINIA, WHICH RULED THAT THE VIRGINIA MILITARY INSTITUTE HAD VIOLATED THE LAW BY DENYING ADMISSION TO WOMEN.

CURRENTLY, NEARLY 11% OF THE CADETS ARE WOMEN.

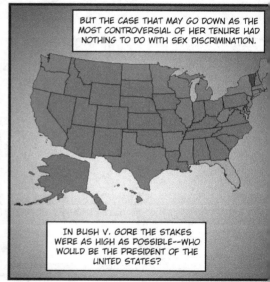

BUT THE CASE THAT MAY GO DOWN AS THE MOST CONTROVERSIAL OF HER TENURE HAD NOTHING TO DO WITH SEX DISCRIMINATION.

IN BUSH V. GORE THE STAKES WERE AS HIGH AS POSSIBLE--WHO WOULD BE THE PRESIDENT OF THE UNITED STATES?

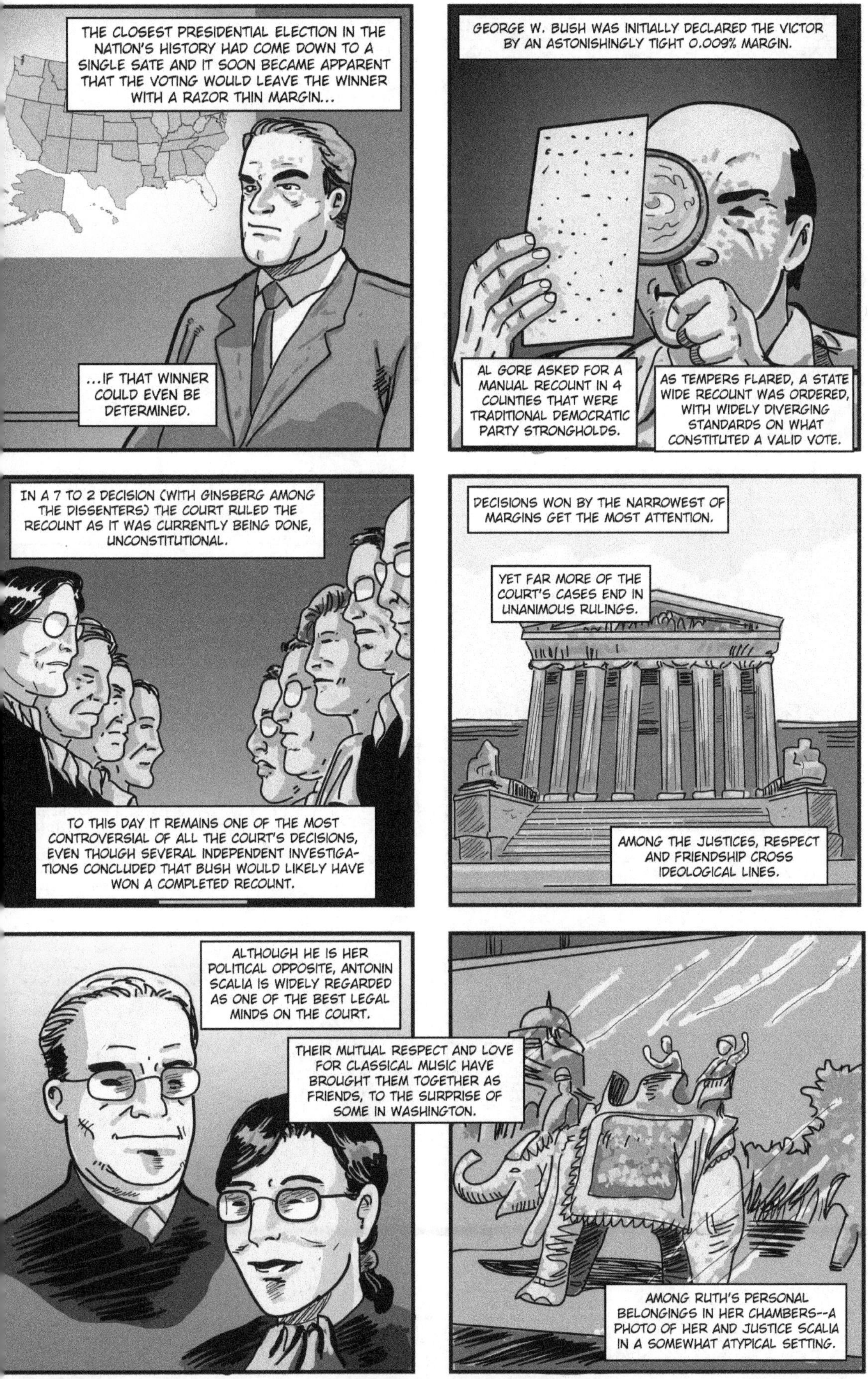
THE CLOSEST PRESIDENTIAL ELECTION IN THE NATION'S HISTORY HAD COME DOWN TO A SINGLE SATE AND IT SOON BECAME APPARENT THAT THE VOTING WOULD LEAVE THE WINNER WITH A RAZOR THIN MARGIN...
...IF THAT WINNER COULD EVEN BE DETERMINED.
GEORGE W. BUSH WAS INITIALLY DECLARED THE VICTOR BY AN ASTONISHINGLY TIGHT 0.009% MARGIN.
AL GORE ASKED FOR A MANUAL RECOUNT IN 4 COUNTIES THAT WERE TRADITIONAL DEMOCRATIC PARTY STRONGHOLDS.
AS TEMPERS FLARED, A STATE WIDE RECOUNT WAS ORDERED, WITH WIDELY DIVERGING STANDARDS ON WHAT CONSTITUTED A VALID VOTE.
IN A 7 TO 2 DECISION (WITH GINSBERG AMONG THE DISSENTERS) THE COURT RULED THE RECOUNT AS IT WAS CURRENTLY BEING DONE, UNCONSTITUTIONAL.
TO THIS DAY IT REMAINS ONE OF THE MOST CONTROVERSIAL OF ALL THE COURT'S DECISIONS, EVEN THOUGH SEVERAL INDEPENDENT INVESTIGA-TIONS CONCLUDED THAT BUSH WOULD LIKELY HAVE WON A COMPLETED RECOUNT.
DECISIONS WON BY THE NARROWEST OF MARGINS GET THE MOST ATTENTION.
YET FAR MORE OF THE COURT'S CASES END IN UNANIMOUS RULINGS.
AMONG THE JUSTICES, RESPECT AND FRIENDSHIP CROSS IDEOLOGICAL LINES.
ALTHOUGH HE IS HER POLITICAL OPPOSITE, ANTONIN SCALIA IS WIDELY REGARDED AS ONE OF THE BEST LEGAL MINDS ON THE COURT.
THEIR MUTUAL RESPECT AND LOVE FOR CLASSICAL MUSIC HAVE BROUGHT THEM TOGETHER AS FRIENDS, TO THE SURPRISE OF SOME IN WASHINGTON.
AMONG RUTH'S PERSONAL BELONGINGS IN HER CHAMBERS--A PHOTO OF HER AND JUSTICE SCALIA IN A SOMEWHAT ATYPICAL SETTING.

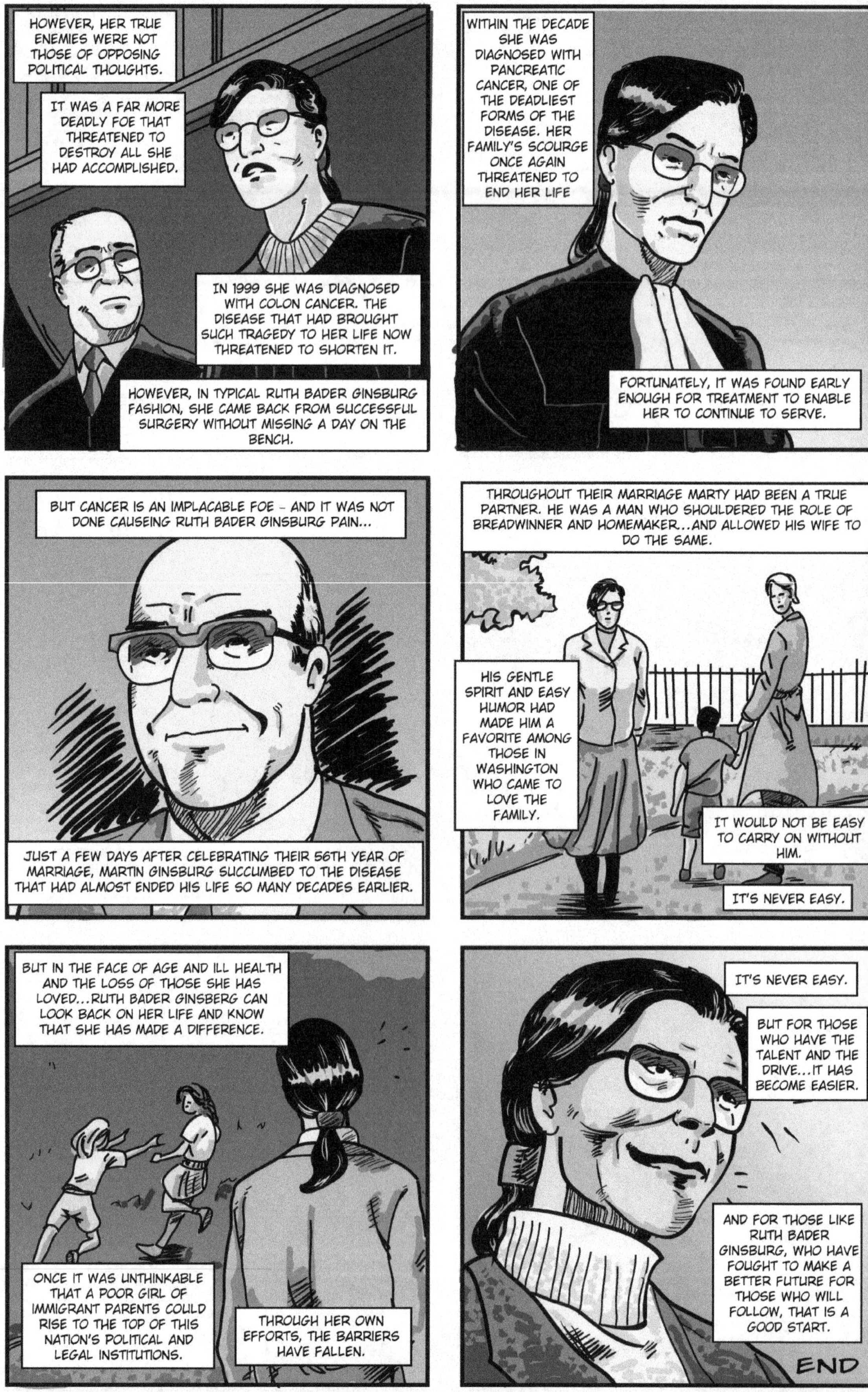
HOWEVER, HER TRUE ENEMIES WERE NOT THOSE OF OPPOSING POLITICAL THOUGHTS.
IT WAS A FAR MORE DEADLY FOE THAT THREATENED TO DESTROY ALL SHE HAD ACCOMPLISHED.
IN 1999 SHE WAS DIAGNOSED WITH COLON CANCER. THE DISEASE THAT HAD BROUGHT SUCH TRAGEDY TO HER LIFE NOW THREATENED TO SHORTEN IT.
HOWEVER, IN TYPICAL RUTH BADER GINSBURG FASHION, SHE CAME BACK FROM SUCCESSFUL SURGERY WITHOUT MISSING A DAY ON THE BENCH.
WITHIN THE DECADE SHE WAS DIAGNOSED WITH PANCREATIC CANCER, ONE OF THE DEADLIEST FORMS OF THE DISEASE. HER FAMILY'S SCOURGE ONCE AGAIN THREATENED TO END HER LIFE
FORTUNATELY, IT WAS FOUND EARLY ENOUGH FOR TREATMENT TO ENABLE HER TO CONTINUE TO SERVE.
BUT CANCER IS AN IMPLACABLE FOE - AND IT WAS NOT DONE CAUSEING RUTH BADER GINSBURG PAIN...
JUST A FEW DAYS AFTER CELEBRATING THEIR 56TH YEAR OF MARRIAGE, MARTIN GINSBURG SUCCUMBED TO THE DISEASE THAT HAD ALMOST ENDED HIS LIFE SO MANY DECADES EARLIER.
THROUGHOUT THEIR MARRIAGE MARTY HAD BEEN A TRUE PARTNER. HE WAS A MAN WHO SHOULDERED THE ROLE OF BREADWINNER AND HOMEMAKER...AND ALLOWED HIS WIFE TO DO THE SAME.
HIS GENTLE SPIRIT AND EASY HUMOR HAD MADE HIM A FAVORITE AMONG THOSE IN WASHINGTON WHO CAME TO LOVE THE FAMILY.
IT WOULD NOT BE EASY TO CARRY ON WITHOUT HIM.
IT'S NEVER EASY.
BUT IN THE FACE OF AGE AND ILL HEALTH AND THE LOSS OF THOSE SHE HAS LOVED...RUTH BADER GINSBERG CAN LOOK BACK ON HER LIFE AND KNOW THAT SHE HAS MADE A DIFFERENCE.
ONCE IT WAS UNTHINKABLE THAT A POOR GIRL OF IMMIGRANT PARENTS COULD RISE TO THE TOP OF THIS NATION'S POLITICAL AND LEGAL INSTITUTIONS.
THROUGH HER OWN EFFORTS, THE BARRIERS HAVE FALLEN.
IT'S NEVER EASY.
BUT FOR THOSE WHO HAVE THE TALENT AND THE DRIVE...IT HAS BECOME EASIER.
AND FOR THOSE LIKE RUTH BADER GINSBURG, WHO HAVE FOUGHT TO MAKE A BETTER FUTURE FOR THOSE WHO WILL FOLLOW, THAT IS A GOOD START.
END

BLUEWATER COMICS

Bill Mulligan — Writers

Zach Bassett — Penciler

Gustavo Rubio — Colorist

Warren Montgomery — Letterer

Warren Montgomery — Inks

Cover: Mike Kilgore

arren G. Davis
Publisher

ason Schultz
Vice President

rred Weisfeld
terary Manager

Kailey Marsh
Entertainment Manager

Maggie Jessup
Publicity

Patrick Foster
Logo Design

Warren Montgomery
Production

BLUEWATER COMICS

www.bluewaterprod.com

PORTLAND'S

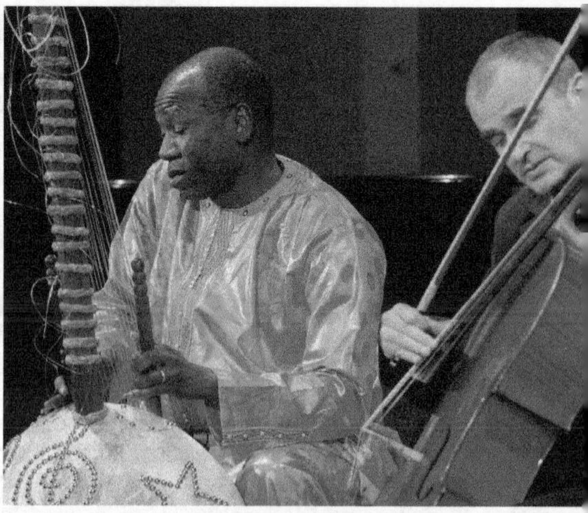

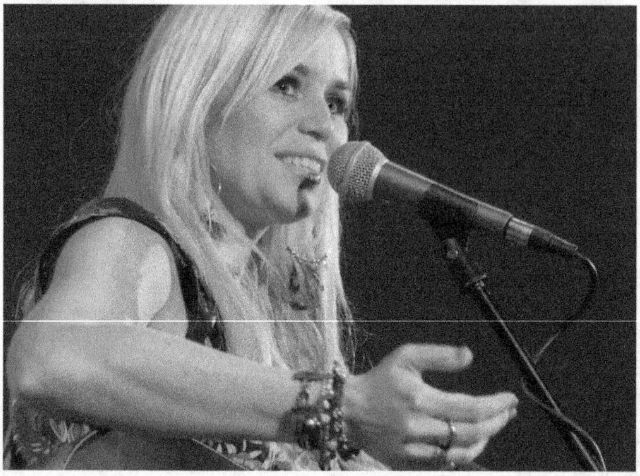

CONCERT

HALL

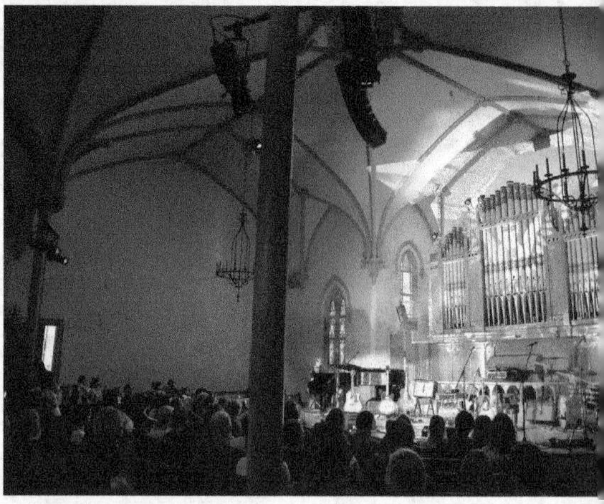

TOC

CONCERT HALL

THEOLDCHURCH.ORG